THE MAKING OF
MODERN LONDON
___1939-1945___
LONDON
AT WAR

To Dad
Merry Christmas
from Marianne + Robert
London 1985.

THE MAKING OF MODERN LONDON
1939-1945
LONDON AT WAR

Joanna Mack
and
Steve Humphries

Sidgwick & Jackson
London

Photographs and illustrations were supplied or are reproduced by kind permission of the following: Associated Press 27, 43, 49/2, 51, 133/1, 133/2; BBC Hulton Picture Library 15/1, 19, 45, 49/1, 54, 68, 69, 91, 93, 108, 115, 152/1, 152/2, 166, 170, 172; British Aerospace 102, 103; Guildhall Library 163, 165/1, 165/2; Borough of Hackney 140; Mary Hankin 114; Bert Hardy 46/1, 60; Elsie Huntley 129; Imperial War Museum 10/2, 33/1, 33/2, 34, 36, 38,39, 42, 62, 66, 82/2, 83/1, 83/2, 89/1, 89/2, 98, 106/2, 111/2, 111/3, 122/1, 122/2, 125, 149, 162, 168; Borough of Lewisham 146; London Fire Brigade 134/1, 134/2, 134/3, 138, 141; London Regional Transport 11, 70, 106; London Weekend Television 32; Vera Michel-Downes 103/2; Museum of London 95, 96; Photo Source 8, 15/2, 22/1, 22/2, 24/1, 26, 58/1, 76, 88, 127, 159; Popperfoto 50, 71, 73, 74, 80, 82/1, 111/1, 118, 128, 154; George Rodgers 58/2; Salvation Army 92; Borough of Southwark 12, 46/1, 46/2; Syndication International 142; Borough of Tower Hamlets 47; Vestry House Museum 64, 148, 156.

First published in Great Britain in 1985
by Sidgwick & Jackson Limited

Copyright © 1985 by London Weekend Television

Picture research by James Barker

Designed by Type Generation
ISBN: 0-283-99232-8 (hardcover)
ISBN: 0-283-99233-6 (softcover)

Typeset by Rapidset, London WC1
Printed and bound in Great Britain by
Biddles Ltd, Guildford, Surrey
for Sidgwick & Jackson Limited
1 Tavistock Chambers, Bloomsbury Way
London WC1A 2SG

For Ann and Fred Mack
and
Sally and Anna Humphries

CONTENTS

ACKNOWLEDGMENTS

We would like to thank all those who have in one way or another helped us in the making of this book. Special thanks are due to Norman Longmate for a detailed reading of the final draft, and to Raphael Samuel for advice on the conceptual shape of the book. We are also indebted to Peter Fryer for his research into the Home Intelligence Reports, and to Terry Monaghan who uncovered for us the story of London's pivotal role in the build up to D-day. Terry Charman of the Imperial War Museum gave us the benefit of his prodigious knowledge of the war, and the museum staff provided much advice and assistance. Dorothy Sheridan of the Mass Observation Archive, University of Sussex, very kindly made much unpublished material available to us. We have also benefited from discussions with a number of other historians who generously gave us their time: they include Angus Calder, Arthur Marwick, Paul Addison, Ken Young, Jerry White, Fred Lindop, Edward Smithies and Rodney Mace.

We are indebted to James Barker for picture research and for all sorts of help with the book. For assistance with finding interviewees, thanks to Tricia Adams, Les Miller, Barry Holliss, Tom Pocock of the *Evening Standard*, Peter Gillman and Paul Couesland and the L.W.T. Community Unit. Many London newspapers have kindly published our appeals for memories, especially the *South London Press*, the *Islington Gazette*, the *Walthamstow Guardian*, the *Hampstead and Highgate Express*, the *Newham Recorder* and the *East London and Hackney Advertiser*. Thanks also to Howard Block of Newham Reference Library and Ian Dowling of East Ham Reference Library, who have both provided us with the benefit of their knowledge of the history of East London.

Thanks are due to many of our colleagues and friends at London Weekend Television. In particular, we want to thank Linda Stradling for her superb work for us, and for helping us overcome the many problems that we have encountered on this project. We are also grateful to Jane Hewland and Mike Chaplin for their comments on the draft chapters. Thanks also to Gavin Weightman, Beverley Spurdens, Pat Newbert, Marcelle Ruddell, Maggie Cook, Derek Murgett and the L.W.T. Photographic Department, not forgetting the superbly efficient L.W.T. Library team, Anne Cornell, Mark Noades, Sarah Adair and Mary Murphy.

Finally, thanks to Harold Frayman and Sally Mullen who have given us a great deal of help and support in this project. And last but not least, a big thank you to the many hundreds of Londoners who have written to us with their stories, some of which appear in this book. We hope we have done justice to their memory of London at War.

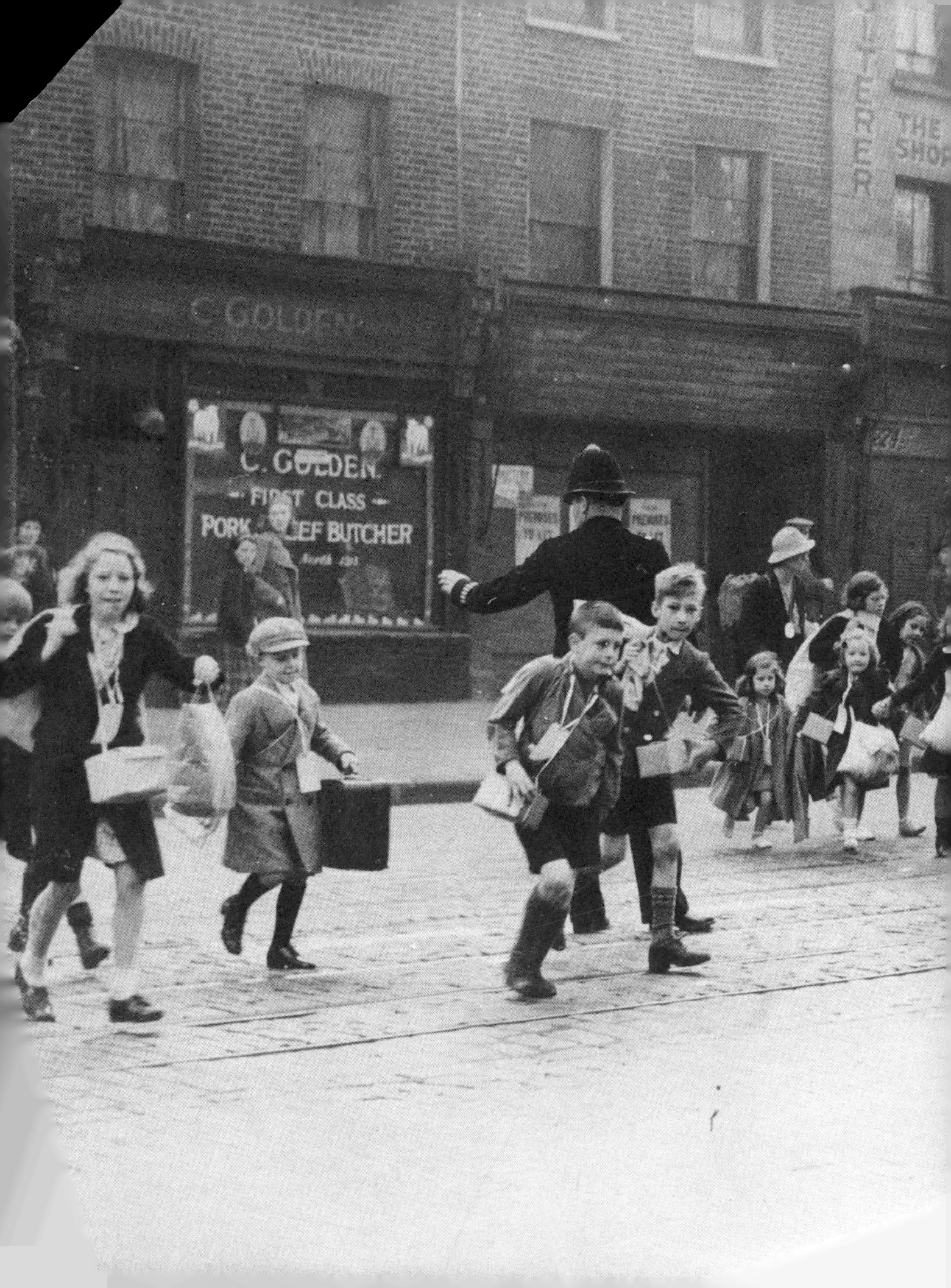
C GOLDEN
C. GOLDEN.
FIRST CLASS
PORK
EF BUTCHER
THE
SHOP

1
IN THE FRONT LINE

In some ways Sunday, 3 September 1939 was just like any other Sunday. Throughout London housewives prepared the family lunch, husbands read their newspapers, young men and women put on their Sunday best. But beneath the familiar routine there was an unusually tense atmosphere. In every home the wireless was switched on. At 11.15 a.m. the voice of Prime Minister Neville Chamberlain came on the air:

> I am speaking to you from the Cabinet Room at 10 Downing Street. This morning the British Ambassador in Berlin handed the German government a final note, stating that unless we heard from them by eleven o'clock that they were prepared at once to withdraw their troops from Poland, a state of war would exist between us. I have to tell you now that no such undertaking has been received, and that consequently this country is at war with Germany.

Londoners felt a strange kind of relief. Britain had been on the brink of war for several months and at last the waiting was over. But there was none of the cheering, flag-waving jingoism that had greeted the beginning of the Great War in 1914. For, though Londoners were pleased that Britain had taken a stand against Germany, they were also deeply anxious. Many commentators had warned that another world war fought with modern weaponry might slaughter millions of civilians and herald the end of civilization. It would come, they predicted, from mass bombardment by enemy air attack. This apocalyptic fear lurking in many people's minds contrasted starkly with the familiar and comforting sights and smells of an autumn Sunday in the capital. People wondered what would happen, what a truly modern war was like, with its new technology of death.

Just seven minutes after the declaration of war it seemed as if they were about to find out. The eerie wail of the air raid sirens sounded over London. Policemen on bicycles pedalled furiously up and down the streets wearing 'Take Cover' placards. There was a stampede to the shelters. People began to run frantically, children screamed, and terrified mothers pushing prams were caught up in the race for safety. Odette Lesley, her mother Marjorie, and her sister Jean, sat in their suburban home in Hendon, awaiting Armageddon:

> I remember when the first siren went, how we struggled with our gas masks, because they were the most awkward things possible to put on. I remember my mother's landed up round the back of her head, I think my sister's landed up on her left ear and, if I remember rightly, it seemed to me somehow that mine landed up on my chest.

Previous pages: The children of Benwell school, Holloway, armed with gas masks, suitcases and sandwiches, set off for an unknown destination in the countryside on 1 September 1939, two days before war was declared

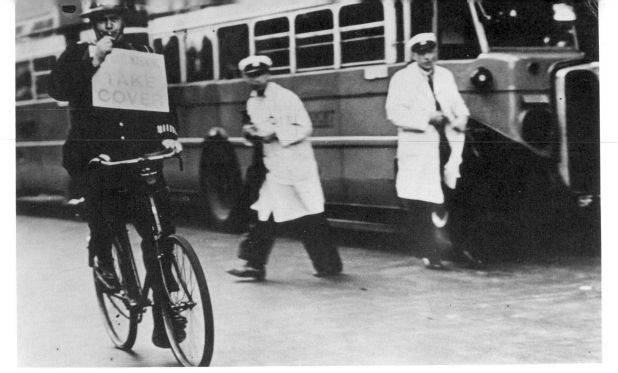

But it was a very terrifying time. We had this awful fear of the air attack on London because, obviously, it was the age of the plane. I used to imagine swarms of planes, always black, with evil-looking pilots in them coming over, raining down death from the sky and I could see buildings all round me collapsing, I could hear screams, terrible noise, terrible panic. Everything was destruction, it was terrible to imagine, and now it became very real in my mind. We thought we were going to get gas raining down. We thought, this is it, we are just going to die.

A policeman warns Londoners to take cover from an air attack just a few minutes after war was declared. It turned out to be a false alarm but it gave the capital a small taste of the terror of total war

Everyone knew that the main thrust of the German attack would be upon London because of its enormous strategic and symbolic importance as the centre of government, communications, trade and industry. Also London, by virtue of its sprawling size, which had doubled during the inter-war years to encompass four hundred square miles, housing eight million people, was a sitting target for air attack. If Germany wished to disrupt the machinery of government, cripple production and break civilian morale, its bombs would achieve maximum impact if dropped on the capital. With the revolution in air warfare which transported death and destruction from the battlefield to the backyard, Londoners realized that they themselves were in the front line.

The powerful German airforce – the Luftwaffe – had been in the forefront of the enormous advance in air technology in the 1930s and its strength was central to Hitler's dream of a worldwide empire. Some experts predicted that hundreds of thousands might die or be injured if the Luftwaffe mounted serious bombing raids on the capital. This danger had prompted the government to make early preparations to protect London against such an attack. For months Air Raid Precautions volunteers had been trained to provide back-up – as firemen, nurses, wardens, and ambulance drivers – should war be declared. A quarter of a million Lon-

doners, most of them part-time volunteers, were now enrolled in the
A.R.P. services. Air raid shelters, usually made out of brick, concrete or
corrugated iron had been hastily built in streets, back gardens, parks and
basements of buildings, and sirens installed to warn of approaching
enemy aircraft.

*Gas mask training in
Camberwell. Everyone, including
babies, was issued with a pig-
snouted rubber mask, for it was
assumed that poison gas would be
dropped in the coming air attacks*

Coupled with the nightmare of air bombardment was the fear of gas
attack. Many Londoners remembered the damage done by poisonous
gases in the trench warfare of 1914 to 1918 and it was assumed that gas
would be used in any future war. The government had issued a handbook
describing in lurid detail how phosgene produced gangrene and how
mustard gas resulted in blindness and decomposition of the flesh. Many
pillar box tops in the capital had been painted yellow with a gas detector
liquid which changed colour when there was poison in the air, thus alert-
ing people to the danger they faced. And everyone, even babies, had
been issued with a pig-snouted rubber gas mask to protect them from the
evil effects of this sort of warfare. Many Londoners had their gas-mask
boxes slung over their shoulders as they sat in their shelters waiting for
the word from wardens to put them on.

To the people waiting, there seemed nothing they could do to stop the
expected holocaust. The government's own plans were based on the
assumption that the bomber would always get through. It was felt that
there was no way of effectively defending London against this new
threat. Many Londoners felt dispiritingly helpless.

But, although on the first day of the war Londoners had a small taste of
what an air attack might be like, it wasn't the real thing. The 'all clear'
soon sounded. A civilian plane had set off a false alarm and an hour later
the shelters were empty. The incident, nevertheless, highlighted the new
role Londoners were to play in the age of 'total war' which would bring
London into the front line of the war. The civilian was to face what only
the military had faced in previous wars. From now on their thoughts and
actions were to be of central importance to the whole course of the war.

As Londoners rushed about on that first day of war frantically making last minute preparations against air attack, the government set about establishing an unprecedented network of official observers monitoring exactly what the 'ordinary' Londoner was doing and thinking. 'Morale' – meaning public attitudes towards the war – became a word that haunted civil servants and politicians. High morale was seen to be of paramount importance in resisting air attack. In order to monitor and manipulate morale, the government immediately set up the Ministry of Information. Based in the Senate House at the University of London, its staff of a thousand had to know what people were thinking. Their strategy was to employ observers to watch ordinary citizens as they went about their daily lives and to report their grievances. This operation was controlled by a new unit called Home Intelligence. Information from all over Britain was gathered, but special emphasis was placed on monitoring morale in the capital.

Londoners had no idea how closely they were about to be watched. Officials of the London Passenger Transport Board, branch managers of W.H. Smith and Sons, supervisors of cinema chains, workers in Citizen's Advice Bureaux, trade unionists, local council officials, social workers, all were to report regularly on Londoners' attitudes towards the war. This information was co-ordinated by regional information officers who also employed full-time observers through Mass Observation, an independent survey organization. These observers supplied regular reports on a wide range of subjects from rumours to anti-German feelings, from gas-mask-carrying to shopping habits. They gathered the information through interviews, observation, and eavesdropping on unsuspecting people's conversations.

Nina Hibbin was a full-time observer in the East End during the early part of the war:

> We tried to get beneath the ordinary sort of 'yes' or 'no' or 'don't know' kind of statement, underneath to what people were feeling. For example, we would not only ask direct questions but we would also ask indirect questions, slipping them into conversations. So I'd perhaps go into a shop and say, 'Five Woodbines, please. Looks like rain. What do you think of the news?' Or we would note down overheards from people's conversations. We had all kinds of rather ingenious ways of assessing morale like, for example, counting how many people had gas masks or how many people we saw in pubs and things like that. Because, if they weren't carrying gas masks they were likely to be feeling happy. If they were feeling rather bad, they'd be carrying the gas masks. From all these sources I'd put together reports on what Londoners were thinking about the war. And the Ministry of Information commissioned various studies, like how people reacted to their 'hush' posters, 'Careless Talk Costs Lives', and things like that, and we did surveys for them on evacuation, and on shelters, and so on.

There were also secret sources of information – police duty room reports and postal censorship. The monthly intelligence reports on morale from Postal and Telegraph Censorship were based on the scrutiny of around 200,000 letters, which were being opened to check on the unintentional leaking of military information. From all these sources of information, the regional information officers produced detailed reports on what people in their area were doing and thinking.

These Home Intelligence reports were highly secret at the time and the material was considered so sensitive that it remained locked away for the next thirty years. Now these records are open to the public and the London Weekend Television team has examined them in depth. They form the heart of the new and controversial interpretation that this book offers of London at War.

From the start, there was a huge discrepancy between these government records of what was really happening and the accounts given at the time by the Ministry of Information and taken up by the press, radio and newsreels. Evacuation is the first major event to highlight this distinction between the official 'myth' and the official 'reality'. The government's mass evacuation plan – finalized in the months preceding September 1939 – was seen as a military counter-move to the enemy's expected strategy of demoralizing the civilian population through air attack, and was presented as a great success for military-style organization. In the first days of war 750,000 Londoners were ferried away in official parties to avoid the expected bombardment. Most of these official evacuees were schoolchildren. Mothers, given only a few hours' notice before the final departure, packed suitcases and sandwiches for their children, tied identity labels around their necks and marched them off to join school groups supervised by teachers. The newsreel and press pictures all showed the mothers happily waving goodbye to their departing children.

But the reality was, perhaps not surprisingly, very different. The mothers, often tearful, found the parting painful. They did not know where their sons and daughters were going or when, even if, they would meet again. The children frequently faced horrendously long train journeys into the unknown. Mollie Matthews, then thirteen, and her sister Joan said goodbye to their mother on Canning Town Station:

> Quite a number of us set off this particular morning, all the mums waving off their children, mine included. Then eventually came the really sad part where we had to get into the carriages and leave our parents behind. The journey seemed to take forever and the awful thing was, as far as we were concerned, that the longer the train was going, the further away from home we were going. It wasn't a very nice feeling. Ultimately the train did pull in at the station, and there we were at our destination. Miles and miles from home, we wondered whether or not we'd ever see our mums and dads again.

When the evacuees arrived, they were gathered together in reception centres. The media talked only of a smooth and efficient finding of homes for this mass of children. In reality, the process was far from smooth. In some places, the children waited days to find a home. In others, a kind of slave market developed in which the children were inspected like cattle. Receiving families would seize upon boys and girls who were tidily dressed

and old enough to help with farmwork or domestic chores, but ignore the raggedly dressed, the weak and the innumerable bands of inseparable brothers and sisters. Doreen Holloway and her brother, William, who had never left Battersea before, now found themselves being looked up and down in Binfield Village Hall in the heart of Berkshire:

> We all stood in a circle with our cases and packages. Some of the villagers came here to select the children they wanted. It got so that my brother and I were left almost till the last and I began to feel most unwanted and rejected because we seemed to be overlooked all the time. Nobody wanted a boy and a girl. At one point a man wanted to take me from my brother and I got very frightened. He wanted to take my clothes out of my case but I stopped him. But we were eventually taken to a home in the village.

The next morning many bewildered and frightened working-class children woke up in strange surroundings in seaside resorts like Lyme Regis or Dawlish, or in distant provincial towns like Taunton. Again this was presented in the press and newsreel accounts as a holiday, a great adventure into the pleasant and healthy countryside. In reality, many children found the experience desperately traumatic.

Back in London, people were also becoming swiftly disillusioned. Now

Nina Hibbin (centre) worked as a full-time 'Mass Observer' in the East End during the early part of the war, providing reports for the government on people's morale

Inset: *London evacuees arrive at Ware, Hertfordshire, in September 1939. Newsreels and newspapers presented a rosy view of smiling schoolchildren, but this was the painful reality behind the propaganda*

that the war had begun, Londoners expected some military action by the Allies. Troop trains chugged out of Waterloo and Victoria Stations taking soldiers on the first stage of their journey to the battlefront, wherever it might be. Crowds of Londoners gathered around maps of Poland in shop windows to work out where the British army might be heading. There had been an air of excitement. But when, on 27 September, Warsaw fell and there was no attempt by Britain and her ally France to provide military support to aid the resistance against Germany, people began to wonder what the war was all about.

On the declaration of war, it had been seen by many Londoners as an epic struggle between good and evil. Since the mid-30s they had received a rising tide of refugees fleeing from the violence and anti-semitism of Nazism. By the end of 1937 almost 20,000 German Jews had entered Britain, escaping from anti-Jewish laws in Hitler's Germany, and the majority had settled in London. Popular feeling against Hitler increased as he extended his empire by annexing Austria in 1938 and then by taking control of Czechoslovakia in March 1939. These conquests resulted in an even greater flood of refugees. In the eighteen months prior to the war almost 50,000 more refugees – many of them Austrian and Czech Jews – had arrived in London. These refugees had been given a welcome by Londoners, who had seen themselves as standing up for basic human rights and against oppression and injustice. Among them was budding art historian, Klaus Hinrichsen who had escaped from Lübeck in Germany:

> I had had encounters with the Gestapo. I could not work in any of my intellectual fields. I was at constant risk of denunciation under the Nuremberg racial laws. We were second-class citizens and when I came to London I had a feeling of relief that I could say what I wanted, that I could behave as I wanted and that, although I was in a foreign country, nevertheless I was accepted as a human being. This friendship extended even to accepting my accent. All the organizations, the Church of England, the Quakers and so on, with whom we had registered, understood the situation and were extremely helpful, extremely sympathetic, and introduced us to English life and institutions. There were lectures put on by the British Council and we got invited to British homes and things like that. I was so happy that now I could join the British in the war against fascism.

Londoners' feelings that the fight was against an evil, aggressive regime had been reinforced in the first days of war by a new wave of refugees escaping from Poland. Popular opinion in London at this time was what might be called 'internationalist': people favoured British military intervention on the side of Hitler's victims, seeing it as a crusade for civilization and basic democratic rights. Though Londoners were desperately afraid of air attack, they nevertheless had an unshakeable confidence that Britain would win, that good would triumph over evil.

But now that Poland had fallen and there had been no action by Britain, people were becoming confused. And as the months went by, nothing else happened; there was a military stalemate at home and abroad. The

German bombers, which had been predicted and prepared for, failed to arrive over London. Hitler's expansion, which Chamberlain's ultimatum had aimed to stop, seemed to have ended – at least temporarily – simply by virtue of Hitler's inaction. He certainly did not seem to want to engage the Allies – at this stage Britain, her Empire and France – in a fully-fledged war. This period of inaction was to become known as the 'Phoney War'.

To many Londoners it didn't seem as if there really was a war on. Because of this feeling of unreality people became less concerned about the dangers they faced and more and more angry at the restrictions imposed upon them by the war. By December wishful thinking had taken over from fear. Many felt that now the capital had had time to protect itself with an array of barrage balloons in the sky and anti-aircraft guns on the ground it was relatively safe; Hitler would probably never dare or be able to attack it. This change in attitude from commitment to complacency shows clearly in the experience of Odette Lesley:

> My mother enrolled us in the A.T.S., and I thought oh, this was mar-
> vellous, I was going to be part of the war effort, I was going to do some-
> thing for my country, I was going to be a soldier. I was absolutely thril-
> led. And I was only fifteen years old at the time, but of course they
> didn't think to ask for a birth certificate, and I hoped they never would.
> And just one month after the war broke out, there we were into
> uniform, mobilised, and sent away to be soldiers. At least that's what I
> thought they were going to do, because I saw myself doing drills,
> learning about guns and holding rifles, and potting away at the enemy.
> But of course it wasn't like that. I was an officer's orderly, making cups
> of tea and generally being a lackey. And in the evenings I'd go out with
> all the fellahs. It was a wonderful time socially but we forgot the war
> altogether, it was just a giggle, nobody took it seriously. After a bit we
> got fed up with the inconvenience and pointlessness of it all and I
> declared my real age – I was dismissed and the A.T.S. had to get along
> without me.

This new complacency helped to undermine the government's evacuation scheme. From the start evacuation had been more painful than was ever admitted, but after three months of Phoney War, it had become a major source of discontent amongst Londoners; though again, this was largely covered up at the time. The main problem was that the parts of London from which many children were evacuated housed most of the poorest families. These children found themselves billeted with provincial or rural families who were often better-off and more 'respectable' than themselves. The result was often a tragi-comic confrontation in which the big city children disrupted many a quiet routine all over the country. The reception families were frequently shocked and disgusted at the poverty of appearance and manners of the London children billeted on them. Late nights, head lice, rough street games, smoking, swearing, chips with everything, bedwetting, some or all of which were common to children from the poorest areas in London, provoked a storm of outrage within the 'receiving' communities. And though most of the 'reception' families tried to be welcoming, many of the evacuees found their middle-class ways terribly formal, and their attitudes snobbish. Sometimes richer households, used to servants, could treat evacuees as second-class citizens. Doreen Holloway, for example, felt totally rejected by the lady who eventually picked out her brother and herself from the Binfield Village Hall 'cattle market':

> The house that we were evacuated to was enormous, at least by our standards. We rarely saw the lady of the house and were put in the care of two servants who obviously resented us. You know, we felt the resentment from the beginning. We had to sleep on sacks filled with straw outside the kitchen, although at the time there were spare beds upstairs in the house. The back garden was rather large but we were not allowed out there, it was out of bounds. My parents were never asked inside when they came to visit us, they had to wait outside the fence in the street. And during one of the meals there the cook actually told me that we were lucky to have the food we were given, as we were eating the same sort of food the lady of the house had. And she made me feel very unworthy and that everything that was going wrong was all my fault. We were not happy at all, we felt really out of place. We felt most unwanted and wanted to get back straight away to London with mum and dad again.

A host of other problems were also developing. Two substantial groups of official evacuees had been pregnant mothers and mothers with pre-school age children. The reception families – and in particular the wives – found it even more difficult to adjust to having a grown-up billeted on them. Although the receiving households were generally better-off, most were far from wealthy, and there was often a shortage of space. Conflicts of culture could consequently turn into a daily drama, from which there was little or no escape into the privacy of separate rooms. Many of the young women evacuees felt lonely and isolated. They had come from the tightly-knit communities of inner London and missed the help of their neighbours.

School-aged children, often parted from their mothers for the first time, also felt homesick. They yearned to get back to the familiar streets of London. Molly Matthews and her sister were billeted in the village of Evercreach in Dorset.

> To start with, the whole environment was so different. We were used to the town and the business and the noise and the country was so different, quiet. And then there was the comradeship, the friendliness of all your friends and your mates that you missed, and the games that we played; silly games really, we used to get tin cans and dent them in the middle and put them on our feet and go round making a huge noise, thinking it was very funny. And all sorts of silly little things that made it home and now no longer existed. It was a strange world and there was no parents around either. We didn't seem to get enough to eat and

it was all part and parcel of missing home too, which I suppose was the basic reason we didn't like the country.

Within a few weeks there was a trickle of evacuees going home – they preferred to face the possibility of attack by the Luftwaffe rather than the life of deprivation in the country. So desperate were some of the children that they ran away from their 'reception' homes, intrepidly making their own journey of tens, even hundreds, of miles back to London.

By December 1939, the aerial bombardment predicted by the government had still not materialized. In addition, the government had by then made parents pay towards the costs of billeting, though people had originally assumed it would be free. Poorer families could ill afford the money. The trickle of returning evacuees turned into a flood. Parents, many of whom were themselves bored and lonely without their children, responded to the unhappy letters which sons and daughters wrote to them and brought them back home. Molly Matthews came back to Canning Town:

> I wrote to mum and dad and explained that we had really had enough by then and if they didn't come to collect us, we would walk home. So consequently we had a letter saying that they would be down that weekend. When they came, they arrived in a taxi. Now I presume it must have taken the best part of their savings, if not all of it. Coaches weren't booked in those days to go anywhere and trains were unreliable, because of all the stations being out of order, so the next best thing was a taxi. So the taxi arrived and the delight, the joy. Then we left and I came home. And I'd rather have faced at home the bombing and things than go back there.

By Christmas 1939 more than half the 750,000 people originally evacuated from the capital had returned. Though relieved at being reun-

A London housewife waits for the bacon coupons to be removed from her ration book. After the rationing of some foods was introduced in January 1940, coupons became a new and often time-consuming feature of shopping in the capital

ited, many families were nevertheless angry and disillusioned with the way they had been treated. A new mood of despondency was in the air.

Feelings of aggravation were heightened by another air-raid precaution – the black-out. From the beginning of the war the government insisted that street and shop lights should be turned off and house windows blacked out with thick curtains, paper and blinds as essential precautions to protect the city from night attack by German bombers. The black-out was unpopular right from the start, partly because it curtailed many Londoners' leisure activities. Floodlit evening sports, like greyhound racing and speedway, were, for example, suspended straightaway. Commuters could no longer read on the blacked-out buses and trains bringing them home from work. Many women became frightened of going out to the cinema, to the theatre or to see friends; fearing harassment, they often stayed at home. Then as the months went by, the rigid legal restrictions imposed by the black-out began to irritate. Wardens, with nothing else to do, were often over-zealous in reporting those who broke the elaborate black-out regulations and the magistrates, anxious to demonstrate their patriotism, too ready to impose fines. There was also a dramatic increase in road deaths, especially of pedestrians, at this time. A Gallup Poll found that eighteen per cent of the population had suffered some accident – bumping into sandbags or lamp posts, being knocked over in the dark, and so on – in the first year of the war. As the phoney war continued, the black-out seemed to be cutting off Londoners from one another and more and more undermining their cheerfulness and confidence.

By the winter another problem, that of rising food prices and food shortages – which particularly affected the poorer sections of London's working class – fuelled the chorus of discontent in the capital. Taxation of items such as beer, sugar, and tobacco – raised partly to help pay for the war – pushed families in places like Stepney and Bermondsey further into poverty. In early January butter, bacon and sugar were rationed. However, the distribution of most foods was still uncontrolled: rich ladies with cars at their disposal could get more than their fair share of unrationed goods by buying from shops in many different areas, causing considerable resentment. The scarcity of goods also pushed up the cost of living, again hitting hardest those on the breadline, often the unemployed and the old. All Londoners, however, were affected to some degree. With the war apparently more imaginary than real, they grumbled bitterly about such deprivations and wondered exactly for what they were being asked to make these sacrifices.

By the beginning of 1940, a deep anxiety had developed in government circles at the rising level of public dissatisfaction and apathy towards the war. The Ministry of Information launched a campaign with the aim of 'replacing public bewilderment with a strong sense of what they were fighting for'. By February all London was festooned with posters displayed in pubs, shops, libraries, tube stations, buses and factories one of which featured Britannia exhorting 'It's up to you'. The M.O.I. film department began to stress in its propaganda shorts the importance of individual effort and vigilance. And to try to overcome the dangerous complacency developing towards the threat of air raids, a booklet, 'How to Make Your Home Safe', was distributed to every householder in London. However, by the M.O.I.'s own reckoning, the campaign had little impact. This had been their first major attempt to change the public's mood and they were still learning the technique of effective propaganda. Morale remained low.

Concern now spread to the Metropolitan Police, who feared that they would be unable to maintain public order and morale after air raids on the capital. They were worried that given the low morale and complacency in London, serious air raids might result in panic, looting and widespread disorder. They were already training their men in the use of fire arms, partly to cope with public disorder. Frank Whipple became a reserve policeman at the outbreak of war:

> We were trained to use arms in case of an emergency in London. They took us out on the Metropolitan Police Range and we were firing old Canadian 1914 rifles. I remember saying to the inspector, 'Who are we going to use these on, the invader?', and he said 'You'll use them on Londoners if you have to. If they get out of control when the invasion and the bombings come you'll have to use them on them'. I remember being quite shocked at the time.

In early 1940 the Metropolitan Police chiefs sent a series of top secret letters to the Army. In this correspondence, which has never been published, the police urged the army to provide them with military back-up able to arrive at any trouble spot in London within one hour of an emergency call. There were already several thousand troops deployed in London whose main role was not originally to defend the capital against a German attack but to 'support the police'. They could regularly be seen patrolling vulnerable points of strategic importance like the docks, arms factories, railway bridges, and aerodromes. There was always a strong presence of soldiers outside the Bank of England, Broadcasting House and the West India Docks. They were there not only to prevent sabotage by 'extremist' groups like the I.R.A., or by German agents and parachutists, but also to avert disorders from Londoners themselves. In the end the Army decided that the military presence already in the capital was sufficient and that it did not have the resources to comply with the Metropolitan Police request. Nevertheless the whole episode illustrates the level of official concern over morale in London at the time.

Then in April a new blow hit morale. Hitler unexpectedly invaded Norway. The British attempt to repel the intruder quickly turned into a fiasco and the military failure was seen by many as evidence that the nation was not geared up for war. The Phoney War was over. But any relief which some might have felt that at last the war had begun, was outweighed by apprehension at Britain's apparent weakness and unpreparedness in the face of Hitler's war machine.

Home Intelligence reported that the 'Norwegian defeat staggered people . . . public morale was at a low ebb. Although there were for the

All change at 10 Downing Street in early May 1940. Neville Chamberlain bows out as Prime Minister after the Norwegian fiasco, and (inset) Winston Churchill takes over to lead Britain into war

first time signs of psychological healthiness: people were facing facts and were not bathed in fantasy. The earlier mood of complacency entirely disappeared.'

But even as the Norwegian debacle was sinking in, a new crisis emerged. On 10 May, Germany invaded Belgium and Holland. Home Intelligence reported an increase in fear, noting that 'anxiety was deepened because it must be remembered that the defence of the Low Countries had been continually built up in the press'. The crisis toppled Neville Chamberlain who was blamed for being a weak leader. Winston Churchill, the First Lord of the Admiralty, was that day chosen to replace him as Prime Minister.

Churchill had been in the political wilderness for many years and was regarded by some as impulsive and erratic, by others as a warmonger. The principal reason that the Conservative-dominated government backed him was because the Labour Party had agreed to take office in a Churchill-led war cabinet, but would not cooperate with Chamberlain. Their support, together with the backing of the trade unions, was essential: a general lack of urgency and commitment had meant that war production had remained at the same dangerously low level as before the war had begun. Churchill's leadership had an immediate effect on popular attitudes towards the war. The 'tough guy' image, deliberately cultivated with the big cigar and the siren suit, his charismatic speeches and his impeccable anti-Nazi credentials all increased the wave of support for him. Through his power and popularity he was able to exercise a decisive influence upon events in London in the spring and summer of 1940. His first speech, declaring 'I have nothing to offer but blood, sweat, toil and tears', set a new tone of determination. The war effort was now beginning to be taken very seriously by everyone.

One of the first acts of Churchill's new government was the formation of the Local Defence Volunteers, rapidly renamed the Home Guard. Tens of thousands of Londoners – some of them First World War veterans in their seventies and eighties – rushed to join this civilian army, and 'do their bit' in their spare time. It was formed to help defeat the dual menace of parachutists dropped behind the front line and the 'fifth columnists', British residents sympathetic to the Nazis who would assist them to sabotage airfields and other key installations. The new technology of the aeroplane, the bomber and the wireless set gave shadowy figures like these an immense power and significance. Reports, both official and in the press, blamed the Nazi successes in Europe on the role of fifth columnists. London's new civilian army seemed to have an important role. To begin with, the Home Guard soldier was only drilling with a dummy rifle, but he felt involved in the defence of the capital against the enemy.

The campaign against potential fifth columnists was heightened by an extension of defence regulations which gave the government the right to imprison anybody believed to endanger the realm. Police quickly arrested members of the British Union of Fascists, and their leader Sir Oswald Mosley. A number of peace agitators and communist activists suffered a similar fate, but the main thrust was aimed at fascists in London.

On 26 May the whole war effort was given a sudden and even greater sense of urgency. Newspapers reported that the British Expeditionary Force of 325,000 men was being evacuated from Dunkirk. Just two weeks earlier, the force had advanced confidently into Belgium to join French and Belgian troops. But the German army had bypassed France's main defence system, the fortress-like Maginot Line, and were advancing at incredible speed towards the coast. The Allies had swiftly retreated. To begin with it seemed that only a few thousand would escape. With the cream of the army and most of its equipment captured, Britain would be defenceless.

However, the next week brought miraculous news. Each day tens of thousands of troops were being rescued by the motley crew of British warships, tugs, trawlers and little sailing ships quickly assembled to bring the beleaguered army back across the Channel to safety. By this time, Belgium and Holland had surrendered, and the Allies lost most of their military hardware.

Dunkirk came as a terrible shock for Londoners. Many of the injured soldiers were taken by train to London for treatment in the capital's hospitals. For many Londoners, the sight of these dishevelled and shaken men pouring into Waterloo Station brought home the nearness of the battle. It had been assumed that the battle would be fought on Continental soil, and, though Londoners had been prepared for rationing and air raids, they were taken aback by what faced them now – imminent invasion. Home Intelligence reported that people were shocked because they had thought the Maginot Line invincible and, before Dunkirk, not one person in a thousand could visualize the Germans breaking through into France. The assumption of an inevitable British victory vanished. The invasion of Britain suddenly seemed likely.

Military chiefs began to implement plans to resist the invasion, which it

was assumed would spearhead on London. The Home Guard helped with a lot of the donkey work, eagerly dismantling signposts, railway signs and any evidence of place names, to confuse the invaders. To stop German troop-carrying gliders using London's roads as runways, vast hoops of metal were erected over dual carriageways and ringroads like the North Circular and the Kingston By-pass. Hundreds of wooden stakes were hammered in rows across open spaces like Hackney Marshes which might be used as enemy landing grounds.

Rich parents who could afford the fares sent their children away in their thousands by liner to the distant parts of the British Empire or to the United States. An official emergency scheme to ship children to safety was swiftly overwhelmed by a rush of applications from middle-class parents, despite the fact that Germany had refused to grant evacuee ships a safe passage.

But the German army, instead of attempting the immediate invasion many Londoners expected, turned south to complete its conquest of France. Everyone, from cabinet ministers to assembly line workers, realized the urgent need to take advantage of this valuable breathing space to replace all the military hardware – tanks, transport, machine guns, rifles and artillery – that the British Army had left behind at Dunkirk. For Britain – and London – to be able to resist Hitler it was crucial that she should be armed. A new effort was also needed so that the nation could be more self-sufficient and export more goods – and with the money earned buy weapons. Munitions factories in the capital began to operate twenty-four hours a day, seven days a week. Many Londoners worked until they dropped. Production rose by a quarter in the week after Dunkirk, and it was sustained at this frantically high level for several weeks to come.

People came to call this new spirit of determined resistance 'the Dunkirk spirit'. J.B. Priestley coined the phrase in his talks on B.B.C. radio referring to the defiant and miraculous evacuation of British troops when all seemed lost. Within weeks this new catchphrase had captured Londoners' imagination as the 'never say die' fight for democracy in which everyone had an important part to play. People all over the capital were saying that this new spirit would get them out of trouble. The 'all out effort' of those first few weeks after Dunkirk certainly boosted the rearmament drive and helped to generate a strong spirit of resistance in London. Hard work and vigilance were to be the watchwords of the summer.

But just as the war effort in London was gaining some momentum and people were resolving to do everything they could to resist the invasion, two more bitter blows had to be contended with. First, on 10 June, Italy, led by the fascist dictator Mussolini, declared war on Britain and France. That night there were riots in Soho with window-smashing crowds seeking early retribution on the Italian community, now seen as another enemy. Then a week later, on 25 June, France, rapidly being overrun by the German army, finally surrendered. Nina Hibbin was out on the streets of East London to record for Home Intelligence people's reaction to this latest blow:

> I have a very vivid memory of the fall of France because I had to go out and, as usual, slip the question in, 'What did you think of the news?' which you just simply couldn't do because on every street corner there were little groups of people, and they were crying. It was the only time I'd ever seen people actually crying in the street. It was not just fear of invasion, it was like, 'That's the end of our alliance, and what's going to happen now?'

Suddenly Britain stood alone – all her Allies had been defeated. Churchill stiffened the mood of resistance with speeches promising 'we'll fight in the fields and in the streets'. These sentiments undoubtedly touched a popular chord and graphically illustrate how the whole attitude towards the war was now completely different from that of September 1939. Then, the war was seen as an international crusade for democracy which Britain would win. Now it was a defensive struggle against the odds, to save themselves from Nazi invasion and enslavement.

The new spirit of resistance which emerged out of Britain's isolation became increasingly insular and xenophobic. 'Now we know where we are! No more bloody Allies!', a tug skipper shouted across the Thames to the writer A.P. Herbert. There was a feeling in the capital that only the British could be trusted in the coming battle. Such feelings found their most extreme form in a sort of collective paranoia or hysteria about the fifth column, the enemy within. It was assumed, first, that fifth columnists had infiltrated London life – Churchill spoke of this 'malignancy in our midst' – and second, that those who had no claim to pure British blood were likely to be the traitors. In short, the foreigner or the 'alien' was not to be trusted. Suddenly, it wasn't just the Home Guard who were on the lookout for fifth columnists – it became a preoccupation of the entire city.

Aftermath of the anti-Italian riots in Soho 12 June 1940, immediately following Italy's declaration of war on Britain. The stoning of Italian restaurants was a sign of the new xenophobia sweeping across the capital at this time

The anxiety was particularly strong in London because, as the capital, it formed the political, military and administrative heart of the nation's war effort. This concentration of power seemed, moreover, to be threatened by London's cosmopolitan nature, by its mass of immigrant groups – Jewish, Italian, Irish, German – which formed more than ten per cent of its total population. This immigrant community had, of course, been 'topped up' by the 55,000 or so German, Austrian and Czech refugees from Nazi oppression who had settled in the capital. Originally they had been welcomed and treated sympathetically. But by the summer of 1940 popular opinion was turning dramatically not only against the Italian community but against the German and Austrian Jews too. Klaus Hinrichsen now found that the warm welcome that the German refugees had first received had evaporated:

> Up to that time the population had been quite extraordinarily tolerant. But once the Germans had started overrunning the Low Countries and Belgium, rumours began to spread, particularly through the press, that German parachutists had descended on those countries dressed as

nuns and priests, and that they'd been assisted by fifth columnists. Suddenly the press, particularly the *Daily Mail* and the *Sunday Express*, took up a vicious campaign against the refugees, suspecting that most of them were fifth column and that they were a danger to the nation. Boarding-house owners suddenly put up notices, 'No Germans, No Jews', which was particularly offensive to the Jews, who had been Hitler's first victims. And I began to be afraid to talk in Underground trains and public places because, although I spoke English, it was quite obvious I was German because of the accent. You could feel that the situation was tense and that it was a fraught situation to run around as an able-bodied young German.

Popular imagination was haunted by images of refugees transmitting information back to the Fatherland on secret radios; of Italian waiters eavesdropping on the conversations of cabinet ministers as they dined in Soho restaurants; of 'foreign' domestics rifling through the secret papers of their high-ranking employers; and of expatriate and German businessmen turned saboteurs blowing up bridges, power stations and aerodromes all over London. The press whipped up this suspicion and hostility, demanding that the government 'intern the lot'.

Internment had in fact begun at the outset of the war when a handful of known Nazi supporters and sympathizers – some of them German – classified as Grade 'A' risks to the nation, had been transported to special camps for prisoners of war. However, the British government maintained a liberal approach and recent immigrants who did not seem to pose any real threat had been classified as Grade 'B' and Grade 'C' aliens and were allowed to retain their liberty. There was a tightening up in May when Churchill ordered the internment of Grade 'B' aliens, but still all the

'Collar the Lot!' 'Aliens' under military escort at Euston Station on 17 May 1940, en route to internment camps on the Isle of Man. Stunning German military successes in Europe fuelled fears that aliens were acting as fifth columnists and undermining resistance to Hitler

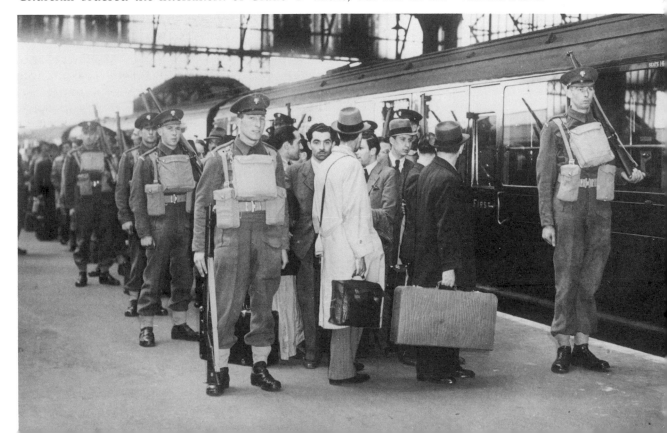

Grade 'C' aliens, which represented the vast majority of recent immigrants, kept their freedom. In June, when Italy declared war, the Italian
community of chefs, waiters, restauranteurs and shopkeepers concentrated in Soho and Seven Dials – many of whom had lived in London for
generations and who identified with the British cause – was also rounded
up. Victor Toliani had lived in London since he was a small child:

> I was brought up in this country, I was educated here, and actually I felt
> like a Londoner. But when war was declared with Italy on 10 June, I
> was arrested a few hours afterwards by Special Branch officers, and the
> shock was enormous. I had no tribunal, no trial, and I was just taken
> away from my family and home, and shunted around the country to
> different prison camps. And the treatment was actually very bad.
> There was one occasion when we were marched through the streets,
> and on a street corner was a teacher with a group of school children,
> and she turned round and said, 'Look at the dirty Germans, spit on
> them', which these kids promptly did. On the other corner was a little
> old lady standing by. She looked at us, and said, 'Well, whoever you
> are, God help you'.

On 24 June panic measures were taken. At Churchill's direction, the
police rounded up and interned more than 15,000 Grade 'C' foreigners
living in London. The vast majority were Jews who had escaped from
Germany and Austria, who would have been sent to concentration camps
by Hitler and who were eager to fight against him. Amongst those
rounded up by the police was Klaus Hinrichsen:

> At that time I lived in a small attic flat in Glenlock Road, near
> Haverstock Hill in Hampstead. One morning very early, came a knock
> at the door and there were two CID officers. They had come for details
> of another German refugee who was living in the house and they asked
> the landlady 'Are there any other Germans in your house?'. She said
> 'Yes, there is someone living on the top floor'. The officers came up and
> told me to get dressed and pack my suitcase. I was just about to go off
> with the Pioneer Corps, which was a non-combatant regiment estab-
> lished for refugees to help the war effort. My call-up was due any day
> and I thought that in fact it was the postman bringing me the note. I
> remonstrated with them and said, 'You cannot possibly take me, I have
> been classified a friendly alien and I am waiting to join the British
> army'. They said, 'You can explain this to our superiors'. They put me
> in the Black Maria outside and I was driven off to Hampstead Police
> Station and later that night to Lingfield Race Course.

In the hysterical atmosphere of this 'collar the lot' campaign all 'aliens'
were arrested, even those who, like Jewish refugee scientists, were playing an important role in the war effort. They were interned in hotels or
hastily converted holiday camps, many of them on the Isle of Man or in
seaside towns, and to begin with they were subjected to a regime which
was often harsh and punitive. Boatloads of internees were quickly

deported to the colonies. Victor Toliani was one of the many Italian internees who were packed into the liner, *SS Arandora Star*, to be shipped to Canada. It was torpedoed in the Atlantic with the loss of six hundred lives:

> Two days out to sea, first thing in the morning, I was still fast asleep under a trestle in the main lounge when a German torpedo hit us. The ship immediately started to list. My friend and I decided to go overboard into the sea, just as the captain was shouting out, 'abandon ship'. This all took place within twenty minutes and the water was already filled with wreckage, and floating bodies. But luckily a raft came by with a person sitting in it, and he helped us into it. We spent ten to eleven hours floating around on this raft, it was like an eternity, and we were sure we were going to die. Then a Canadian destroyer came along and picked us up.

Summer 1940 was a time of seeking for scapegoats in the capital. 'Foreigners', who wanted to contribute to the war effort, found themselves excluded. A number were dismissed from their work, rejected by the Home Guard or turned out of their homes, whether they were council or privately rented. Even refugees from Britain's former allies, Belgium, France and Poland, were harassed and were highly unpopular at this time. Home Intelligence reports noted that in Richmond there was 'growing anti-alien feeling leading to refusal to allow Belgian refugee children to join play centres; shop assistants becoming insolent to people with foreign accents; refugees expressing fear'. In Hammersmith and Dulwich there were 'people booing Belgian refugees in the street'. Because London was such a cosmopolitan city huge numbers of its people were afflicted in one way or another by the atmosphere of suspicion and division. For example, the Home Intelligence reports on Finchley record cases of 'victimisation of British subjects bearing foreign names'. The witch hunt was extremely divisive and even loyal British citizens were interrogated by the police and shunned by neighbours if there was the slightest suspicion that they were fifth columnists. This happened to Odette Lesley:

> I came home one night to the flat where I lived in Hampstead and found that the police had broken in. They started to interrogate me in an awful sort of way, saying things like, 'You're an enemy agent, you're a fifth columnist, whose paying you?' And this interrogation seemed to go on for such a long, long time, until I realized what had happened. I had left a light on without drawing the black-out curtains and, of course, it was shining out like a beacon across the Heath which to them was a signal to the enemy, because it was thought that this sort of thing was being done by fifth columnists. I realized the awfulness of what I'd done. Imagine me signalling the enemy. Eventually I did convince them that I was not an enemy agent, it was a pure accident and in the end I was just fined two pounds at the local magistrates court. But the outcome of it was that many of the neighbours around shunned us

for quite some time, whispering 'Look, fifth column', which was to me so dreadful because nobody was more anti-Nazi than I was.

The whole episode of mass internment was also, as it turned out, completely unnecessary. The reports of the key role of fifth columnists in the downfall of Europe were either fabricated or grossly exaggerated. Hitler had not used the refugee migration to Britain as an opportunity to 'plant' spies as was widely suspected. The fifth columnist in London was a complete myth.

In July 1940, however, Londoners awaiting the inevitable German invasion found the fifth columnist theory a comforting explanation of Hitler's remarkable military success, as did the defeated Allied generals. It offered the hope of some sort of control over the coming conflict and of resisting the Third Reich, if only they were vigilant enough to weed out the enemy within. For by this time Hitler had developed a superhuman reputation: he and his war machine appeared infinitely cunning, immensely strong and almost invincible.

Despite the growing spirit of resistance in the capital, some were none too optimistic about Britain's prospects. The official scheme to evacuate children to the Empire continued to be flooded with applications. Churchill moved in to try to stem the tide of panic, winding down the evacuation scheme to avoid a stampede out of the country as he believed this would be very bad for morale. And he orchestrated a new campaign using propaganda films and posters – the silent column campaign – to root out any traitors in the ranks who might be spreading alarmist and defeatist talk. In fact, the campaign proved counter-productive, deepening the atmosphere of suspicion and uncertainty in the capital. Anyone, whoever they were and whatever their background, became potential objects of suspicion. There was a spate of prosecutions for careless and defeatist talk as police and informers tightened their grip on comment and criticism of government action. After only a week, this had led to serious discontent in London. The Home Intelligence reports for London record 'many people feeling nervous about anti-gossip campaign and that they are afraid to open their mouths'. Londoners were saying that the policy was 'turning us into a nation of spies'.

Most of the rumours were, in fact, attempts to find out the truth of what was happening. People were aware of rigid censorship, they distrusted the press. They often listened to the Nazi chief English language broadcaster, William Joyce – popularly known as Lord Haw Haw because of his haw hawing upper-class voice – to get the other side of the news. It was understandable that in such circumstances rumours – for example, that the royal family and government were about to evacuate to Canada – were rife. The whole anti-rumour campaign caused such bad feeling that it had to be abandoned at the end of the summer.

The main problem which concerned the British government at this time, however, was one of high level strategy involving the defence of Britain, and especially London, against invasion. Throughout the summer British Intelligence desperately tried to piece together scraps of information to predict the invasion date.

The search was given even more urgency in mid-July when Hitler announced, 'I have made a decision to prepare for and if necessary carry out an invasion of England.' His plan was to establish a bridgehead on the south-east coast between Folkestone and Worthing and to advance on London, the capture of which, he thought, would end British resistance. A Gestapo 'hit list' of thousands of London notables, featuring ministers, politicians, civil servants, industrialists and journalists, was created, plans were made to remove national treasures – including Nelson's column – to the Fatherland, and a scheme was drawn up to transport men of working age to camps in Europe.

The people of London, knowing that they were to be the main target for the coming German onslaught, prepared for a last stand. Churchill declared that we would 'fight for every inch of London, down to the last street and suburb'. Londoners comforted themselves with the thought that resistance would be strengthened by the presence of the evacuated British Expeditionary Force and by a new wave of conscription which brought another 500,000 into the armed forces. Most of these troops were to be deployed in mobile forces to attack the Germans when they arrived and advanced from their coastal positions. They would have been aided by a secret plan to drop mustard gas on the invaders as they landed on the beaches. In the south they aimed to prevent the enemy crossing a 'stop line', which ran all the way from Maidstone in Kent to the Bristol Channel.

The defence of London itself lay in the hands of a number of battalions of the regular army and the Home Guard. Together they prepared three lines of defence around London (see map on page 32). The first two, on the outskirts, were anti-tank lines with deep trenches, barriers, pill boxes and road blocks. The outer line circled London's suburban frontiers linking together Rickmansworth, Potters Bar and Epping Forest in the north with Hounslow, Kingston-upon-Thames and Bromley in the south, bordering Uxbridge and Yiewsley in the west and Redbridge and Woolwich in the east as part of its grand sweep around the capital. The next line of defence ran several miles inside this outer barrier linking together Enfield to the north, Harrow to the west, West Norwood in the south and Wanstead in the east. The third inner line of defence was bounded to the south by the River Thames, and to the east and west by the Rivers Lea and Brent with the circle finally meeting to the north at the Dollis Sewage Works. This inner line was seen to be crucial to the defence of London, and was to be wholly manned by the regular army. Finally, a last stand was planned in the Whitehall area by crack troops like the Royal Marines and the Scots and Grenadier Guards. Machine guns were placed inside or on top of strategic buildings, and on street corners all over the area. Rapidly erected pill boxes were often disguised as tea stalls. Contingency plans were made for special protection to be given to notables like the royal family, the Prime Minister and leading government officials; they were to be flown away to safety if the enemy advanced this far and if the fall of London looked inevitable.

The Home Guard was to play a key role in the defence of London's two outer anti-tank lines. It was stressed at the time that these lines should be

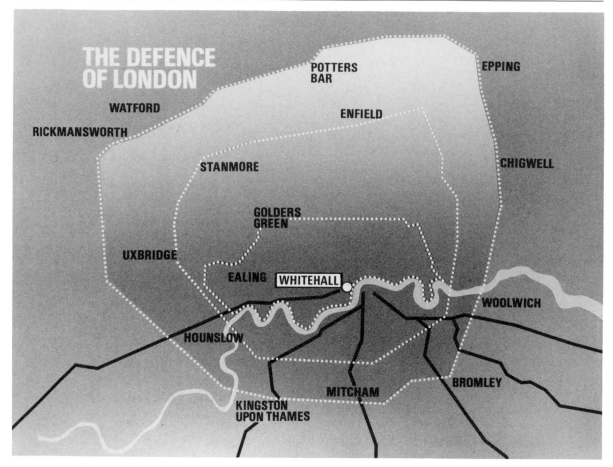

THE DEFENCE
OF LONDON

POTTERS
BAR

EPPING

WATFORD

RICKMANSWORTH

ENFIELD

STANMORE

CHIGWELL

GOLDERS
GREEN

UXBRIDGE

EALING   WHITEHALL

WOOLWICH

HOUNSLOW

BROMLEY

MITCHAM

KINGSTON
UPON THAMES

The three defence lines round London which were to resist the German invasion should it come. The first two, on the outskirts, were anti-tank lines with deep trenches (one of which ran the length of Epping Forest), pill boxes and road blocks. The inner defence line of pill boxes was bounded by the Rivers Thames, Lea and Brent

held to the last man – no withdrawal was permitted without direct orders from headquarters. The efforts of those volunteers, who spent their evenings and weekends practising techniques of schoolboy naivety to sabotage tanks, shooting from uncovered positions at imaginary German planes, or laying trip wires across the roads – thereby threatening local drivers more than the Germans – have been affectionately parodied in 'Dad's Army'. For these first few months, the Home Guard was controlled by the old officer class, of whom there was an abundance in the London area, and who were often bungling and out of date in their military experience. They would train the men in traditional drill and trench warfare instead of more useful and effective guerilla tactics. Self importance and 'little Hitlerism' led to a number of motorists being shot at road blocks. Lack of care as well as lack of experience, resulted in injuries and fatalities when using firearms. All this gave the Home Guard the reputation of being the only army ever to kill more of its own men than the enemy. It is certainly difficult to envisage this ill-equipped and ill-trained civilian army of clerks, retired bank managers and ageing colonels holding up Hitler's advance. Len Jones, a member of the 57th Surrey Home Guards Unit, was preparing to prevent any enemy advance across the Mitcham part of London's outer defence line:

Disguised pill boxes sprang up all over the capital in the summer of 1940, most of them appearing on London's three defence lines. Left: *A petrol station façade hides a pill box strategically placed opposite the level crossing at New Malden, Surrey.* Below: *An innocent-looking hut on the north side of the Chelsea Bridge masks a pill box within*

Below: *Hastily improvised barricades made of earth, wood and derelict motor cars in Tolworth, Surrey – part of London's outer defence line. It was hoped that barricades like these would halt the advance of the German panzer divisions on the capital*

We were told to dig great anti-tank trenches across the sewage farm by Hackbridge Junction. The plan was that the tanks would fall into them and they would be so steep that they wouldn't be able to get out. We thought this was a waste of effort, so we only dug shallow trenches and covered them over with branches so the top brass wouldn't notice. Another plan we had was to creep up on the German tanks at night when they were still, kill the sentries, and plant sticky bombs on the caterpillar tracks so that when they started up next morning they would explode and dislocate the tracks. Then, when they got out of the tank to repair it, we would throw sulphuric acid balls at them. Our favourite sabotage tactic, though, was trip wires. We practised stretching wires between trees. We were going to use that trick to get German motor cyclists as they went along the road – if they had been going fast, the aim was to take their heads off.

Though the great invasion fear had brought out a stoic determination, people's efforts were at this stage still badly organized. This stemmed in large part from the inefficiency of the old school of traditional civil servants, officers and employers who were in charge of the war drive in London. For example, the directorate of the Home Guard at first banned some younger men who had fought in the Spanish Civil War from joining on the grounds that they were politically suspect and too left wing. A number of these Spanish Civil War veterans, like Tom Wintringham,

A 'Dad's Army'-style exercise in which a tame-looking home-made tank is set ablaze by Home Guard defenders wielding Molotov Cocktails – petrol-filled beer bottles – in the late summer of 1940

nevertheless set up a new school at Osterley in Middlesex to train Home Guard units in guerilla techniques – for instance, the use of Molotov Cocktails to demobilize tanks, camouflage and street fighting. The school proved extremely popular with London's Home Guard recruits. But the Home Guard command wanted the school closed down, explaining that their men did not have to do 'any of this crawling around; all they have to do is sit in a pill box and shoot straight'. Though the popularity of the school did ensure its continuation, these official attitudes hampered its work.

Inefficiency was also great in industry. Labour relations had admittedly improved since Churchill had taken power, a change partly due to his recruitment of leading figures from the Labour movement like Ernest Bevin, Clem Attlee and Herbert Morrison into his new cabinet. But the Conservative-dominated cabinet prevented any sweeping measures to take control of industry and direct labour. As a result the 'take-off' of the war economy was more disorganized than it need have been. Many women – for example in Harrow, Richmond, Dagenham and Woolwich – who had responded to government propaganda and volunteered for war work, found there was little or nothing for them to do in their area. The Home Intelligence reports record, for instance, that in Harrow the Labour Exchange Manager was finding it 'difficult to pacify spates of women wanting to undertake war work'. The Labour Exchange in Hampstead employed belittling tactics to deny Odette Lesley the war work that she wanted:

> I very desperately wanted to do war work, I was dying to do my bit, but instead of that, what did I land up doing? Cleaning out rabbits and working as an animal attendant for the Medical Research Council in Hampstead! I thought it was a terrible waste of time. I begged the Labour Exchange to let me do war work, maybe in the Land Army or whatever sort of job. And they turned me down, they just took one look and said, 'Good Lord, a shrimp like you, you couldn't do any-thing!' and of course I could have done, because I was strong and heal-thy. The frustration I felt was absolutely awful, but I could do nothing about it, the authorities had the last word.

There were similar feelings of resentment amongst former workers of the luxury and sweated trades in places like Stepney and Bethnal Green, who were forced into unemployment by the slow and chaotic switchover to war production in the capital.

While all this labour power was wasted, those in employment, espe-cially people in the aircraft industry, working for example at Hawker's in Kingston and Napier's at Acton, were often urged to work round the clock. This proved to be counter-productive. When output began to drop in July due to overwork, illness and fatigue, Bevin had to reduce the maximum number of hours to be worked a week to sixty in order to pre-vent people burning themselves out.

The summer also saw the futile 'saucepans into Spitfires' campaign, initiated by Lord Beaverbrook, the Minister for Aircraft Production. Mil-

Two Royal Marine sentries with fixed bayonets guard the Admiralty Building overlooking Horse Guard's Parade in 1940. It was in this area that a last stand was to be made should Germany break through London's three defence rings

lions gave valuable kitchen utensils but the publicity stunt backfired when it was realized that they didn't contain sufficient aluminium to be useful. The result was enormous dumps of saucepans in scrapyards and a shortage of saucepans in the kitchen.

Leading advocates and publicists of the Dunkirk spirit – in particular, broadcaster J.B. Priestley and the *Daily Mirror* under crusading proprietor Cecil King – were highly critical of the injustices and inefficiencies in the way the war was being run. Partly as a result, increasing numbers of Londoners felt that it should be more of a 'people's war' and that the old privileged class of Colonel Blimps, as they were dubbed, was getting in the way.

But, despite the failures to channel effectively the 'Dunkirk spirit', the mood in London in the summer of 1940 was much more positive than it had been at the outbreak of war. The fears then of a massive air attack on London had engendered a feeling of helplessness. The visions now of Nazi divisions attempting to march upon London had, by contrast, created the feeling that there was an active role for everyone. Commuters bought guerilla warfare booklets on station bookstalls and middle-class women in places like Hampstead formed private armies teaching themselves weapon handling. Government leaflets advised civilians to stand firm, demobilize motor cars and give no assistance to the enemy. Every Londoner had a part to play in the defence of the capital. From this mood emerged an exhilarating feeling of self-confidence. The Home Guard, for example, believed that they really could stop the massively well-equipped panzer divisions of the German army, as Len Jones remembers:

Most of the men in the unit worked in engineering and we could use all the latest engineering equipment, so we managed to improve beyond recognition all the old weapons we got lumbered with in the Home Guard. The old Smith guns we were given were very crude, but we machined new barrels and fitted sights onto them to make them very accurate. We modified the sten guns we were given to make them more accurate, and our stock of bayonets and knives we made razor sharp. And we made our own acid bombs and sticky bombs. We really thought we could stop the German army. In hindsight, we weren't aware of how difficult it would be to get anywhere near the German troops and tanks without being killed, but we felt that our dogged determination would get the better of them.

This feeling of confidence was given a tremendous boost during the summer of 1940 by the success of the R.A.F. For, before the Germans could invade, they had first to gain control of the air over Britain. On 13 August the Luftwaffe set about the systematic destruction of R.A.F. Fighter Command, in the air and on the ground, as the final stage in Hitler's invasion preparations. The Battle of Britain, as the air war between the R.A.F. and the Luftwaffe came to be called, was close-run. Many British pilots were killed and the Germans nearly destroyed a vital ring of seven aerodromes around London. The Luftwaffe was, however, held at bay, and this resistance was heralded as a major triumph in the propaganda of the time. The R.A.F. seemed to most people, including Churchill, to be winning the day.

The Battle of Britain was, however, not so much being won, as changing course. In the last week of August, a few German raiders, who had lost their way, emptied their bombs on the capital by mistake and in direct contravention of Hitler's orders. Though small in scale, this seemed to be the sort of targetting of the London population which had been so feared and expected at the outbreak of war. On subsequent nights, the R.A.F. bombed Berlin. The German response was to shift from military to civilian targets. On 4 September Hitler proclaimed, 'In England they're filled with curiosity and keep asking "Why doesn't he come?" Be calm. He's coming. He's coming. When they declare that they will increase their attacks on our cities, then we will raze their cities to the ground.'

But Londoners now believed that the R.A.F. had mastery of the air. Their fears, which had so dominated the outbreak of war, had receded just at the time when the Battle for London was about to begin.

2
THE BATTLE FOR LONDON

Saturday, 7 September 1940 is day etched into the memory of many East End families. At around five o'clock on a hot, summery afternoon they were drawn onto the streets by the approaching roar of several hundred bombers. Most of them thought the planes were British for they had come to believe that the capital was no longer vulnerable to such an air attack.

Then the bombs began to fall, first on the Arsenal in Woolwich, then thousands raining down on the vast complex of docks on both sides of the Thames – especially the Victoria & Albert, the East India and the Surrey Commercial – setting them ablaze.

Very quickly people crouched in the official street shelters, or in their own living rooms, realized that they too were targets as the maze of narrow streets and blocks of flats from West Ham to Bow, from Bermondsey to Whitechapel and from Limehouse to Poplar were blitzed. One of those standing in King Street, Poplar was eighteen-year-old Len Jones.

> That afternoon, around five o'clock, I went outside the house, I'd heard the aircraft, and it was very exciting, because the first formations were coming over without any bombs dropping, but very, very majestic; terrific. And I had no thought that they were actually bombers. Then from that point on I was well aware, because bombs began to fall, and shrapnel was going along King Street, dancing off the cobbles. Then the real impetus came, in so far as the suction and the compression from the high explosive blasts just pulled you and pushed you, and the whole of this atmosphere was turbulating so hard that, after an explosion of a nearby bomb, you could actually feel your eyeballs being sucked out. I was holding my eyes to try and stop them going. And the suction was so vast, it ripped my shirt away, and ripped my trousers. Then I couldn't get my breath, the smoke was like acid and everything round me was black and yellow. And these bombers just kept on and on, the whole road was moving, rising and falling.

The first wave of bombs was hitting the poorest and most overcrowded parts of London and some slum buildings, like the jerry-built tenements of Canning Town, disintegrated into rubble, burying their occupants underneath. In the shelters, there were men and women shouting and screaming hysterically as each blast rocked the very structures that were protecting them. London was experiencing its first mass air attack by the Luftwaffe.

The East End faced the full brunt of this attack. The first instinct of Gladys Strelitz and her family in East Ham was to run away from the bombs:

We had been bombed all day long and there was a lull. My brother said, 'Come on girls, get all the children's clothes in a bag and we've got to get out of London, there is a lull'. And so we got this bus, and we went to Bow. And when we got to Bow the bombing was going so badly that the conductor pulled the bell and said that we wouldn't go any further. So the only place to go was to run under this crypt, under this big church. And there the sight that met my eyes, it overcome me. Because there was people praying, and crying and asking God to help us, because there was bombs going on and this crypt, it was actually shuddering. And, well, it was too much for me, I just passed out.

Len Jones ran into a nearby street shelter in Poplar, which he was to share with several Chinese families that lived in the area:

The shelter was brick and concrete built, and it was lifting and moving, rolling almost as if it was a ship in a rough sea. And the suction and the blasts coming in and out of this steel door, which was smashing backwards and forwards, bashed us around against the walls. The extent of injuries at that stage was just abrasions really, the shoulders and chest getting crushed against the wall, or across the floor. The worst part was the poor little kids; they were so scared, they were screaming and crying, clutching at their parents. The heat was colossal, the steel door was so hot you couldn't touch it. And everybody was being sick and people were carrying out their normal human needs, and the smell was terrible.

The second attack came later that evening and continued into the early hours of Sunday morning. By this time 430 East Enders had died – many corpses lay in the streets and gardens. Sixteen hundred were seriously injured, and tens of thousands were made homeless. Len Jones was shocked by what he saw when he emerged from his street shelter early that morning:

I went out to see how our house was, and when I got there the front door was lying back, and the glass of the windows had fallen in, and I could see the top of the house had virtually disappeared. Inside, everything was blown to pieces, you could see it all by the red glow reflecting from the fires that were raging outside. Then I looked out the back and suddenly I realized that where my father's shed and workshop used to be, was just a pile of rubble, bricks. Then I saw two bodies, two heads sticking up, I recognized one head in particular; it was a Chinese man, Mr Say, he had one eye closed, and then I began to realize that he was dead.

When firemen like auxillary Bill Ward arrived at the docks, they faced a uniquely terrifying spectacle:

We go into Surrey Docks and the flames are all over the place. There's telegraph poles alight, the fences were alight and, when we get nearer to the canal, there's even barges alight. Everything was alight including the warehouses, and everything inside them was burning, the fumes choked you. We'd have to walk in the middle of the road because the Germans overhead were flinging down the bombs and walls and masonry were falling everywhere. I don't think any firemen had ever seen anything like it before.

Flames engulf the Surrey Commercial docks, as the first bombs rain down on Black Saturday. In a few hours the fires will be declared out of control

London's inexperienced fire brigade declared the massive conflagration in the docks out of control. Blazing warehouses poisoned the atmosphere with their flaming contents: pepper, rum, sugar, wood, paint and rubber. Armies of rats, forced out of the warehouses by the fires, roamed the glass-strewn streets. At times it seemed as if whole dockland communities would be surrounded and engulfed by fire, but firemen working non-stop for two days managed to keep exit routes open for the worst hit areas.

During and immediately after these attacks the emergency services almost broke down. Nurses in the ill-equipped first-aid posts dotted around the East End were besieged by the walking wounded. Ambulances found it difficult to get through the bomb cratered streets to ferry the seriously injured away to hospital. Weary rescue squads – swamped by the magnitude of the devastation – worked furiously to free as many of those trapped in the debris as they could. The next morning some homeless families wandered aimlessly around the ruins of their shattered streets while others formed long queues outside the rest centres provided for them. Bombed-out families, desperate for food, clothing and shelter, were bewildered to discover that practically no provision had been made for them.

The dominating memory of that first and awful night of bombing –

Devastation in Selsey Street, Limehouse, in the aftermath of the Black Saturday air attack. Rescue teams worked day and night to free people buried in the rubble and to clear the streets

known locally as Black Saturday – is one of shock, panic, helplessness, confusion and hysteria. Although the true horror was covered up by the press, the nightmarish experience has remained with many East Enders for the rest of their lives. It seemed as if it was the end of the world. Gladys Strelitz recalls, 'As we got out of the crypt, we could see the Home Guard actually digging out bodies. And the smouldering flames and the stench was terrible and the sky all lit up with flames. It was a terrible sight. Shattering to reveal it, to remember.'

Len Jones remembers the horror of finding his neighbours:

When I saw the dead Chinese, I just convulsed and couldn't get my breath. I was shaking completely. Then I thought well I must be dead, because they were, so I struck a match, and tried to burn my finger, I kept doing this with a match to see if I was still alive. I could see, but I thought I cannot be alive, this is the end of the world. The fires were everywhere and everything you looked at was red, sheer heat, blood, the lot. That night haunted me for more than forty years, it was so awful I couldn't tell anybody about it, it almost destroyed me.

Some of the panic that night was caused by the Army. It seemed possible that the mass bombing, combined with favourable moon and tide conditions, could mark the beginning of Hitler's long-awaited invasion. The code word 'Cromwell' – which meant that the invasion was imminent – was signalled around Britain. This was widely interpreted as meaning that the invasion had actually started. The Home Guard were called out and in one part of Eastern Command the Army blew up strategic bridges. All this added to the confusion in the East End as fire-fighters were warned to look out for parachutists and fifth columnists.

Hitler did plan to invade Britain – but not yet. The plan, code-named Operation Sea Lion, depended on first destroying R.A.F. Fighter Command and on undermining the nation's will to resist with a ferocious bombing campaign. Both had to be achieved quickly, for he needed to invade before the winter set in; otherwise bad weather could ruin his plans and the invasion barges gathering in north-west France and Belgium would be a sitting target for the R.A.F. The blitz on London which began on Black Saturday was to serve this dual purpose: to lure the British air force out for a final battle to the death, and to soften up or possibly to knock out London by bombing her civilians into submission. Black Saturday marked the beginning of a phase which was to have a crucial military significance. In fact the Battle of London, as the first major wave of bombing on the capital is known, had a bearing on the whole course of the war.

On Black Saturday and the first few days and nights of bombing which followed, many Londoners felt defenceless. There were few British fighters protecting them against the ravages of the Luftwaffe. They had no way of knowing that Fighter Command had lost so many planes in the previous month of air battles that most of the remaining fighters had to be deployed to protect airbases from further attacks. The sudden mass attack on London did catch Fighter Command by surprise but even in its immediate aftermath they could only muster a limited defence of the capital. In a sense the blitz on the people of London gave the R.A.F. valuable breathing space, for their own aerodromes were no longer being bombed.

Londoners were also disturbed by the fact that there was at first little anti-aircraft fire deployed against the raiders. Fortunately, perhaps, people did not realize that the sound location equipment on which the gun crews relied to locate their target had proved, at this, its first real test, totally ineffective.

The feeling of terrible vulnerability was heightened by the government's failure to make adequate preparations for the protection of London's civilians during air raids. Civilians had never before had to bear the brunt of a mass enemy air attack, but government experts, basing their predictions on isolated incidents during the First World War and the bombing of places like Guernica in the Spanish Civil War, predicted that hundreds of thousands of Londoners would either be slaughtered or would suffer from hysteria and neurosis. Because the destructive power of the air raids was grossly overestimated, many authorities in the capital made all the wrong preparations for the attack. Millions of cardboard coffins and preparations for quick burial in quicklime proved – mercifully –

largely redundant. So, too, were the teams of psychiatrists who were on standby to provide therapy for mass neurosis. What Londoners did need, and what was hopelessly inadequate, was decent shelter. In some areas like West Ham there were hardly any shelters at all. This shortage was aggravated by the fact that almost all the 750,000 London evacuees, whom the government had hoped would spend the war in the safety of country towns and villages, had drifted back into the capital since the mass evacuation of September 1939. Also, it had been wrongly predicted that air attacks would be by daylight and would be over fairly quickly, which meant that shelters had no provision for people to sleep or eat and inadequate toilet facilities.

There were several different types of shelter. One of the most effective 'domestic' types was the Anderson shelter: it was like a miniature Nissen hut, made of corrugated steel, sunk three feet into the ground in the back garden and covered with earth. Two and a quarter million Andersons had been provided free by the government before the blitz. Now that people were spending the night in these shelters, they found that the Anderson had an irritating tendency to leak and flood, and that conditions inside were extremely cramped. But the Anderson quickly proved itself able to withstand practically anything but a direct hit. People sheltering inside were protected from falling rubble and flying glass and as a consequence many lives were saved. The main problem was that Andersons were garden shelters; and many Londoners had no gardens.

As a result, in the East End few families had Andersons. Hundreds of

Free hand-out of Anderson shelters in Islington, February 1939. These corrugated iron shells had to be sunk in back gardens, so many Londoners with no gardens had to do without

Below: *The street shelter in Parkstone Road, Peckham Rye, September 1940. From the outside these brick and concrete shelters didn't look very sturdy or safe, and many Londoners used them only as a last resort*

Above:*Inside the Parkstone Road street shelter huddled families – many feeling helpless and dejected – waiting for the bombs to fall*

brick and concrete street shelters, each one holding about fifty people, had been erected in nearly every street in the area. Government efforts to save cement and confusingly drafted instructions had, however, resulted in some being shoddily built with inadequate mortar. Most East Enders didn't like the look of them; they were cold, dark, smelly and looked shaky. When the bombs rained down, their worst fears were realized. Roofs and walls frequently caved in, sometimes even when the bomb blast was some distance away, and collapsing buildings sometimes buried shelterers alive. Emily Eary swiftly became concerned about the danger of official shelters in the Aldgate area:

The warning had gone, we all ran to the shelter. There was my Mum, my two sisters and my brother. We ran down the stairs, and we all sat huddled together on a form. It was very cold, damp down there, and there were crowds of people. Then the bombers came over, and in the early hours this bomb came down, it whooshed down. We didn't know where it had hit, we just sat there. It shook the shelter, we were covered in dirt and dust, it was choking everybody and we all got into a bit of panic. We couldn't move, we just sat there. Everybody was saying, 'What's happened, what's happened?'

Then we realized that the buildings had had a direct hit, collapsed onto the entrance of the shelter, and we couldn't get out. And we had to crawl out the far entrance. We were crawling over old forms that people had turned over to get out in a panic. We crawled to the end and as we got out we saw daylight, and we saw a big space where our flats had been. There were many people killed down there, but we were just relieved to get out that day, and wondered where we were going to go next night.

Southill Street, Poplar, shattered by bomb damage, September 1940. London's East End took the brunt of the first few days and nights of saturation bombing

The anger of East Enders would have been even greater had they known that their counterparts in German cities had been provided with huge, comparatively luxurious bunkers, many of which boasted separate rooms, toilets, washrooms, and sometimes even electric elevators.

London's East End took the brunt of those first few days and nights of saturation bombing between 7 and 11 September. Its familiar cityscape of terraced rows, warehouses and factories was, in just four days, shattered by bomb blast and fire into what looked like a smouldering shanty town. Whole streets were reduced to rubble. The horror of it all and the feeling of defencelessness created a sense of shock and panic.

Many families abandoned the official street shelters, rushing around desperately searching for shelter wherever they could; under railway arches, in warehouses, in crypts, or in the churches themselves – which were believed to have some sort of holy immunity to bombing – and in overcrowded and insanitary bunkers.

The panic was carefully concealed in the press which spoke only of noble and heroic resistance. But it is clearly revealed in the top secret Home Intelligence reports to government chiefs, which show what was really happening. The Home Intelligence report for 9 September noted that: 'In dockside areas the population is showing visible signs of its nerve cracking from constant ordeals.' On the next day it reported: 'Increased tension everywhere and when the siren goes people run madly for shelters with white faces. . . . Bermondsey Citizen's Advice Bureau is inundated with mothers and young children hysterical and asking to be removed from the district. . . . Exodus from East End growing rapidly. Taxi drivers report taking party after party to Euston and Paddington with belongings.'

Thousands of terrified East End families trekked out of London. They struggled through cratered streets, pushing babies in prams, the elderly in wheelchairs and their possessions loaded in hand carts. Gladys Strelitz recalls:

> The day after, well, we came out of the crypt and everybody was fleeing for their lives because it was still blazing. And we got the children and we knew we got to run for it like everybody else was running out of London. You had to escape, so we just managed to get into a baker's van that took us to the station. And we decided to go to Maidenhead and take the children there.

Refugees also fled to Epping Forest in Essex, Reading, Windsor, Oxford, and to the Kentish hopfields, where they camped out under the trees or in makeshift wooden huts. Mary Price set off with her young baby.

> There was destruction and flames and smoke everywhere and the noise was terrible. We were petrified. We didn't know where to go and what to do. The only thing we could think of was to get to Kent to the hopfields. At least we'd be safe getting out of London. Some cousins of mine came round; they'd borrowed a lorry and they said, 'Come on,

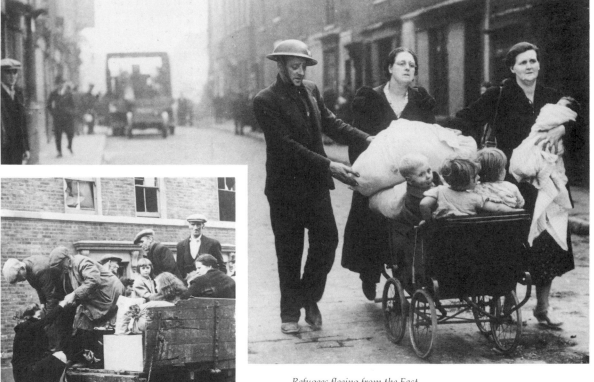

*Refugees fleeing from the East
End in the first days of the blitz.
Above: Mothers and children,
escorted by a warden, begin their
trek to safety outside London.
Left: Families load their
belongings onto a lorry en route
for the hopfields in Kent*

we're going' and I just took two bags of clothes with the baby. I had a
five-month-old baby.

We made our way to Kent. It was just like a convoy of refugees going
out. Everything on wheels, old cars, old lorries, anything that moved,
it was one steady stream going towards the coast. We got to the hopfields and there's this wonderful sense of peace, nothing was happening. We slept in the huts on straw that the farmer provided.

This mass exodus recalled the flood of disorganized refugees that had
crippled French resistance and had blocked military manoeuvres in
Europe a few months earlier. The British government feared a repeat performance and had army units waiting to control and stop the refugees on
their way out of the capital.

However, some official attempts to bring an atmosphere of greater calm
by organizing the evacuation in an orderly fashion went disastrously
wrong. West Ham Council, for example, gathered several hundred
people – mostly homeless mothers and children – who wished to be

The remains of South Hallsville Road school, West Ham. On the night of 10 September 1940 around 400 people – many of them mothers and children – perished when a bomb scored a direct hit on the school. The families were waiting to be evacuated. It was the biggest civilian disaster of the war

evacuated in South Hallsville Road School, Canning Town, which had no air raid shelter. The coaches to take the refugees away were directed to Camden Town instead of Canning Town, and while the women and children waited overnight, the school suffered a direct hit which killed almost everyone inside.

The growing sense of vulnerability in London was reinforced by a widely-held belief that the authorities could not be trusted to tell the truth about what was really happening in the war – and, in particular, the cost to London of the blitz. The government took the view that the sight of death and destruction on London streets, or the knowledge of its extent, would have a demoralizing effect. Thus any film or photograph showing deaths from an air raid was banned, and press reports on casualties of bombings were censored. The M.O.I. stipulated that any film of a bombed-out street had to end with a building that was intact. It was forbidden to give the names and localities of damaged buildings for twenty-eight days. This cover-up process was completed by the body disposal squads, whose job it was to collect quickly the shattered remains of dead bodies and transport them to mortuaries.

There were, of course, sound military and psychological reasons behind all this. In particular, it prevented German military chiefs from calculating how damaging their air raids were and which targets had been knocked out. However, the official silence did fuel pessimistic rumours

Blankets cover the remains of bomb victims in Holborn during the first weeks of the blitz. Photographs like this, which showed death on the streets, were banned for fear of undermining civilian morale

and undermined people's confidence in the reliability and honesty of the British press and newsreels. Even if people did not have any direct experience of death and destruction in their family and neighbourhood, they could see the evidence of it when they travelled to work or to the shops. The strange new landscape of bomb-blasted buildings told its own story. And where censorship prevented an official explanation, Lord Haw Haw and German black propaganda radio stations like the 'New B.B.C.' moved in to provide horrific imaginary details of the damage done. Censorship was a breeding ground for suspicion and rumour, and during the first few days of the blitz there were plenty of demoralizing rumours that London was about to grind to a standstill.

But the main reason these rumours gained a widespread currency was that, in those first few days of the blitz, they seemed believable. The East End did appear to many of its residents to be moving towards chaos. In particular the main provision for the homeless – rest centres – were proving to be disastrously inadequate. The principal problems were severe overcrowding and insanitary facilities. In one rest centre in Stepney – a converted elementary school – three hundred people had the use of ten pails and coal scuttles as lavatories. Though most of these families had been bombed out, the overcrowding was further aggravated by the arrival of temporary evacuees. Hundreds of unexploded bombs littered the streets waiting to be defused, which meant that whole communities had to be evacuated and all roads closed within a three-hundred-yard radius of each bomb. The handful of troops which had been trained to deal with bomb disposal had received only the most basic training. Bert Woolhouse was a sapper with the Royal Engineers:

When we went out on a bomb, we used to draw lots to see whose turn it was to be in the hole first. And we used to evacuate the area around for three hundred yards and we were very inexperienced, didn't know hardly anything about bombs or explosives, and we were young – only 'squaddies' – and I can assure you that we were very, very frightened when we got into a bomb hole on our own.

On this particular occasion, when we were digging the bomb, we found a fuse which we knew was an anti-handling fuse and then, when we tried to get this bomb out, it exploded. I was thrown many yards, and covered with rubble and my ears were bleeding. I was crying and a chimney pot hit me on the head. All my comrades were killed, blown to pieces. The most found of anybody was a piece of leg in a Wellington boot.

The tragedy and chaos of those days and nights were made worse by widespread looting. While fire brigades continued to struggle bravely to contain each conflagration, and heavy rescue squads tried to dig out survivors, the bombed and evacuated buildings provided rich pickings for looters. There was often a narrow line between 'helping yourself' and criminal activity. Children would rummage through rubble looking for salvageable items, and some poor families would ensure that they had enough food by lifting it from shops with their fronts blown in. Sometimes policemen and civil defence workers would 'rescue' goods which, they argued, were about to be destroyed. Petty criminals took advantage of the dark streets and empty houses to steal goods for the black market which was now growing fast as shortages began to bite. Frank Whipple, a reserve policeman, patrolled the dock areas, 'There was a terrible lot of looting. You'd find bent wardens, heavy rescue men, even police doing it. People were like vultures, going into bombed-out houses and shops, and they'd even take rings and valuables off dead bodies. We would have to accompany them to the mortuary to stop that happening.'

Reports of such incidents were censored, but a lot of people knew what was going on: shopkeepers found their stocks depleted after raids and families found their prized possessions missing from their damaged houses. For many, suffering already from the strain of the raids, this seemed to be the last straw. When Gladys Strelitz returned to her home, having evacuated her children, she was in for a shock, 'We went home to find that all around us was shattered. We had just had our windows blown out, but people had been in and looted my home and all the bed linen and everything was stolen and, well, we were full of despair. It was sad enough leaving the children, but to come home to that.'

On 11 September Churchill tried to raise people's flagging spirits with a speech broadcast to the nation. Londoners, huddled around their wireless sets, heard the Prime Minister tell them that the barges for the invasion lay in wait across the Channel. He described the Luftwaffe's attempt to win air mastery as 'the crux of the whole war'. He said that the week that followed would rank in British history 'with the days when the Spanish Armada was approaching the Channel and Drake was finishing his game of bowls; or when Nelson stood between us and Napoleon's

Grand Army at Boulogne'. He finished, 'every man and woman will therefore prepare himself to do his duty whatever it may be, with special pride and care'. Although some Londoners greeted the speech with cheering and many were moved by it, there was still deep government concern that their morale was cracking.

This concern peaked on the fifth day of the blitz – 12 September – when thousands of East Enders stormed tube stations in East and Central London to use as shelters. Officials had rejected the use of the Underground for this purpose fearing that those inside would develop a 'deep shelter mentality' and would lead a troglodyte existence, never daring to come to the surface until the war was over. Also they wished to keep the Underground railways clear so that movement of troops, the injured and the evacuated could be carried out under London without hindrance. But when the idea that the tubes could provide a safe refuge from the bombing took hold of the popular imagination there was a stampede to the stations which officials couldn't stop. Sheltering in the tubes began when hundreds of families bought tickets, rode the trains, then evaded station staff in a bid to stay on the platforms all night. But after a few days, crowds just brushed past the police and London Transport officials trying to keep them out. Emily Eary and her family were amongst them:

When we got down there we would travel the tubes. And the porters, the station staff, used to say, 'Clear out, get out, you're not supposed to be down here', so we would travel, just pretend we were travellers, just to be down there, because we knew it was illegal. When the trains stopped running, we'd put our bits and pieces, our old blankets and our pillows on the platform and we'd lie there against the wall.

But gradually, it just caught on, and people were so frightened they had to force their way down. They were determined that they weren't going to be thrown out. People would rush to the tubes, almost knock you over to get down the escalator because when bombs were coming down, people were getting panic-stricken to get out of the noise and the devastation.

People camped where they could – on the platforms, in the corridors, even on the stairs. Though the authorities disapproved, they found themselves powerless to move the swelling crowds. Within days more than 150,000 people were taking refuge in the safety of the tubes.

The very way in which the Underground system had been taken over by the people, against the wishes of the authorities, became symbolically important. It signalled the beginning of an attitude of self-reliance and community initiative that was to help build a new spirit of resistance in the next, and critical, weeks of the blitz.

This emergent mood was reinforced by the commencement of an intense barrage of anti-aircraft fire. British night fighters were withdrawn and London's anti-aircraft guns, which bristled across Hyde Park, Battersea Park and Richmond Park, had the opportunity to blaze away at the bombers. General Pile, the ack ack commander, issued orders that every possible gun should fire, however remote the chances of hitting any-

Londoners bed down for the night on the escalators at Piccadilly Circus tube station, late September 1940. Despite authorities disapproving, about 4,000 shelterers took refuge at this station each night

thing. The terrible noise that the resulting barrage made kept many people awake all night. The shells, in fact, killed far more civilians – through falling fragments – than German pilots, while unexploded shells added to the chaos already caused by unexploded bombs. However, people did not realize all this and the thunder of British guns, which at least forced enemy aircraft to fly higher, gave a boost to Londoners' morale. Also, now that the Luftwaffe's new strategy of relentless bombing of the capital had become clear, Fighter Command deployed many more aircraft to protect London. At last it seemed something was being done to defend the city. The panic and anarchic exodus of the first days was dramatically reduced.

But the British defences could not stop the bombers. The Luftwaffe kept coming through day after day, and in greater strength night after night. While the eastern riverside boroughs – from Stepney to Canning Town and from Bermondsey to Deptford – continued to take the brunt of the attack, the more central areas of the City, the South Bank and the West End were now also beginning to be heavily hit.

In the front line in the fight to withstand this saturation bombing and to keep London ticking over stood the emergency services. The fire service played a critical role because of the widespread use of incendiary bombs. Fires, many times worse than any confronted in peacetime London, blazed every night. The burden of fire-fighting fell on the 2,000 professional firemen of the London Fire Brigade, backed up by the 23,000 full- and part-time auxiliaries called up at the beginning of the war. The volunteer firemen came from many backgrounds: bus drivers, labourers, journalists, artists, salesmen, and a number of conscientious objectors. In the long lull prior to the blitz they had been openly derided by the public as 'war dodgers, loafers and parasites'. As a result many left the service and from June 1940 the government had to stop any more men from resigning in order to maintain the fire service's strength.

The fires now threatening to engulf whole communities and reduce built-up areas to ashes gave the firemen the opportunity to answer their critics and to end the stigma of cowardice. This they did in the most emphatic way. They battled night after night against the flames, often not sleeping or resting for days. The danger they faced from collapsing walls, falling masonry and poisonous fumes, was made more horrifying by the fact that their work was often done in the thick of air raids. The Luftwaffe often preceded a major bombardment with an incendiary attack, causing widespread fires which formed easily identifiable targets for their bombers. As a result, hundreds of firemen, were killed or injured on duty.

Despite the nightly ordeals which confronted firemen, there were only a handful of canteens to provide them with food and drink while they fought the fires. Some ended up drinking polluted water from the Thames for refreshment. Those who survived serious injury would arrive home suffering from conjunctivitis, numerous cuts to face and hands, burns, dehydration, and body sores from the continuous chafing of perpetually wet uniforms. Yet, still they would turn up for duty the next day. For the part-timers – who worked one night on duty, one night on call and one free – there was the added burden of going straight to their civilian jobs the next morning.

Many factors drove London firemen – the majority of whom had no previous experience of fire-fighting – to make these sacrifices. The desire to prove their courage and endurance in the face of public hostility was initially a potent factor. It was quickly replaced by a desire to live up to public expectations for, after a few days in the front line, the London firemen became folk heroes. They could now expect cups of tea from housewives and might be cheered as they drove back to the station. Some firemen clearly thrived on the excitement and exalted sense of purpose which had before been absent from their humdrum lives as clerks, labourers or factory workers. For others the opportunity to be in the centre of the action was far preferable to the nagging tension and strain of sitting at home or in a shelter wondering where the next bomb would fall.

But probably most important in stiffening their resolve for the terrible risks that lay ahead was the solidarity with the firemen who worked alongside them. This comradeship was fostered by mutual dependence. Their lives and the lives of those they were trying to save depended on a high level of trust and teamwork between crew members. Wherever a fireman was, whether perched eighty feet above a turntable, hosing water down on to a blazing building, or surrounded by fire in a crumbling warehouse, he was never completely alone. Bill Ward, an auxiliary in the

London Fire Brigade, was each night in the thick of the fires, 'Well, you knew you were both in the same boat. If he died, you died. If he lived, you lived. Everyone depended on everyone else. So there was great comradeship there. You knew that every man there was going to try to look after you and keep you safe, and you'd do the same for them.'

A similar esprit de corps also developed in other groups. Rescue squads dug out the living and the dead from bombed buildings. Many of the rescuers had been building workers – bricklayers, plumbers, carpenters – who used their knowledge of construction techniques to salvage what they could from the ruins. Stretcher carriers lifted the injured away from bombed-out buildings. Doctors performed endless operations on blitz victims. Repair gangs worked round the clock attempting to restore broken electricity cables, sewage pipes, gas mains and telephone cables. All these groups had to brave the bombs which rained down day and night, hampering their work. They all played a key role in keeping London going and making some sort of civilized routine possible. Many were professionals but, as with the firemen, there were also large numbers of volunteers from all walks of life.

At the heart of the air raid defence system was the air raid warden. A network of thousands of air raid wardens, nine tenths of whom were voluntary part-timers, covered the capital. On average there were ten per square mile. Their job was to report incidents, call up the appropriate rescue services and, if they were first on the scene, to do their best to rescue the trapped and provide first aid for the injured amidst the debris of the raid. They also had the dangerous task of investigating unexploded bombs. In the first days of the blitz a number of wardens had shown themselves to be totally incompetent – some had even run away. Those who remained, together with new recruits, provided for the most part an invaluable service to their local communities.

Women made a crucial contribution to maintaining essential services during the blitz. Because this was very much a civilian's war and because there was such a shortage of manpower, there were many opportunities for women to become involved in all sorts of A.R.P. and civil defence work. Many thrived on this new freedom. About one in six wardens were women, most of them middle-aged housewives who carried out their duties on a part-time voluntary basis. Women also volunteered in large numbers to drive fire engines and ambulances – in fact, most of London's ambulance drivers were women. This was a popular option amongst the more prosperous, for the ability to drive was at this time relatively rare. They faced unprecedented dangers, driving in virtually pitch darkness – only dimmed sidelights were allowed – along hazardous cratered streets strewn with glass and rubble. For June Buchanan, Society 'deb' turned ambulance driver, the contrast with life before the war could hardly have been greater:

> There was such a remarkable difference between my life on and off duty. When I was off duty, I'd be shopping in the West End, dining at the Ritz, wearing smart dresses, going to balls, generally enjoying the social scene in London that I'd just been introduced to after I was pre-

sented to the King. Then on duty, I'd do my shifts twelve hours a day, driving the ambulance to and from incidents in my plain cotton coat and cap – it was a completely different world. We all just did what we had to do. I'd often find myself carrying the dead and injured on stretchers into the ambulance and rushing them back to hospital along the blacked-out streets. I just took it in my stride. The bombs would be falling all around, but you felt better out doing something to help rather than waiting for them to drop on you.

Many women also acted as despatch riders, often risking life and limb on their motor cycles to deliver important messages in and out of heavily bombed areas. And women played a key role in maintaining communications in the capital – usually by telephone, staffing emergency control centres during the blitz. This was often more dangerous than it sounds, for it meant working through air raids to ensure the coordination of emergency services.

But probably the most arduous and exhausting job performed by women in the front line was nursing. State registered nurses were bolstered by thousands of auxiliary nurses who were given only a few weeks' emergency training, often with the Red Cross or the St John Ambulance Brigade. They provided care and comfort for the injured in air raid casualty wards, at first-aid posts, and in bombed-out houses where heavy rescue teams searched for survivors. The conditions they worked in were often primitive, overcrowded and dangerous. When they were working alongside rescue teams, they were sometimes lowered down through narrow holes in the rubble to give morphine injections to those buried beneath. For all this they received just 25 shillings a week – barely enough on which to survive.

The example of calm and courage set by the emergency services and the order that began to emerge out of the chaos as a result of their efforts, helped to foster a growing stoicism amongst Londoners. Indeed, the government was startled that when they hastily revived their evacuation scheme for children it was not taken up en masse by London families. Many mothers preferred their children to remain at home during the bombings rather than face another upsetting evacuation. When the heavy bombing began on 7 September there were around 500,000 children of school age in the London evacuation area, but by the end of September only 20,000 unaccompanied children had been evacuated despite official encouragement. Here was clear evidence that people were adjusting to the challenges of air attack.

Even those who had been bombed out and lost practically everything seemed to be coping better with the crisis. In the first days of the blitz many had simply panicked. Now people could often be seen on the day after the bombing carefully going through the wreckage of their homes trying to salvage the remains of their possessions. Commentators noted that finding small personal belongings seemed to help people through the ordeal. Some would recover enough to recreate the feeling of home in a corner of the shelter where they spent their nights. Others would gain immense relief from learning that their pet canary or parrot had survived

Left: *Little Londoners armed with gas masks and suitcases about to board a train bound for the country, 26 September 1940. Only 20,000 unaccompanied children were evacuated on official schemes by the end of September – one sign that the capital was coping much better with the air attacks*

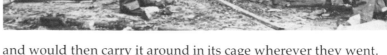

Right: *Members of the Home Guard – armed with truncheons to prevent looting – have a cup of tea with A.R.P. workers outside blitzed shops in the Old Kent Road, October 1940. The 'cuppa' took on an almost magical significance during the blitz*

and would then carry it around in its cage wherever they went.

Those who had not been bombed out often took treasured family items, like wedding photographs, and practical things, like brushes or a spare pair of shoes, to the shelters with them. If their homes were hit then these would become prized possessions – a link with a familiar past – giving them greater personal strength.

When all seemed lost there was always the cup of tea. People were observed going back to their homes to find the windows blown in and splinters of glass everywhere, and proceeding calmly to put the kettle on for their morning 'cuppa'. The propaganda films of the blitz regularly played on this routine to illustrate people carrying on as normal. Tea acquired almost a magical importance in London life. And the reassuring cup of tea actually did seem to help cheer people up in a crisis.

But new crises continued to emerge. The first stemmed from the damage and destruction wrought on thousands of homes by the bombings. For those at home, the conditions that people had to put up with – especially in the worse-hit East End where a third of the population was able to remain in their houses – were often rather primitive during these early days of the blitz. Suddenly people who were getting used to a world of running water, electricity, and wireless sets were plunged back into Victorian conditions. Most houses suffered some sort of damage in the first few weeks of raids even if this amounted only to shattered windows and cracks in the ceilings and roof. This, together with the regular cut-offs in the electricity, gas and water supplies, made any sort of normal family life impossible.

At the same time there was a host of problems emerging from the lack of adequate shelter. One solution taken by some Londoners was to return to the habits of their early ancestors and to live in caves. They discovered the existence of a set of caverns at Chislehurst in Kent and, as with the London Underground, they simply broke into them. Families each took over a small section. Sometimes double beds, armchairs and tables were transported down in carts and lorries. After a week of the blitz more than 8,000 Londoners were living in these caves. Most were homeless families and older people who had no work to go to, but some commuted daily to their offices and factories in central London.

But the worst conditions were to be found in the mass shelters in the East End where there was appalling overcrowding. The largest and most notorious – the Tilbury shelter – was a massive underground goods yard beneath the Tilbury railway arches in Stepney. It housed as many as 14,000 to 16,000 people each night, all of them jam packed, head to toe, lying on the concrete floor. Less privileged and poorer groups, especially Indians, Maltese, West Indians, Jewish refugees and prostitutes, slept in particularly dirty and smelly parts of the warehouse amongst trodden excrement and soiled margarine. Every afternoon massive queues waited outside the 'Tilbury' and when the doors opened there would be a mad scramble for the better places. Nina Hibbin, as an employee of Mass Observation, was responsible for providing regular reports on the 'Tilbury':

> The first time I went in there, I had to come out, I felt sick. You just couldn't see anything, you could just smell the fug, the overwhelming stench. It was like the Black Hole of Calcutta. There were thousands and thousands of people lying head to toe, all along the bays and with no facilities. At the beginning there were only four earth buckets down the far end, behind screens, for toilets. It was terribly hard on the old people because they were obviously terrified. They'd usually come down in their pyjamas and dressing gowns and they'd have to sit up all night huddled together. The place was a hell hole, it was an outrage that people had to live in these conditions.

Overcrowding also became especially bad in many of the tube stations. People had to sleep as best they could in cramped and uncomfortable conditions, on floors and against walls. Platforms were packed tight with bodies, people slept on the escalators and slung hammocks over the rails – the power was turned off after the trains had stopped running at 10.30

p.m. There was often no sanitation or washing facilities on the platforms and people walked down the tunnels to relieve themselves. The stench was dreadful and in the older Underground stations a plague of mosquitoes thrived on the heat and the unwashed bodies.

Though these deep shelters were grim and unhealthy, their main advantage was their relative insulation from the noise of bombings and the feeling of safety – not always justified – that they engendered. As a result people were able to sleep a little better in them than in the much more vulnerable surface shelters, where sleep was practically impossible. However, even in the tubes, only three or four hours' sleep would be snatched each night.

The Tilbury shelter, a massive underground goods yard in Stepney, in October 1940. Each night it housed as many as 16,000 shelterers in conditions of appalling overcrowding and squalor

This dramatic change in home life – the private suddenly becoming much more public – provided a severe test for the resistance of East Enders. The inconvenience and discomfort of it all provoked arguments and complaints. Yet there was a tremendous adaptability to hardship. The bombings in those early days of the blitz, concentrated as they were on the eastern riverside boroughs, had hit hardest the poorest, working-class districts of the capital where the people were quite used to accepting deprivations. They had a strong sense of humour and, even more important, a strong spirit of community solidarity. Mary Price returned from the hopfields, driven back by the cold weather and she found this neighbourliness flowering in the tube shelters:

The only thing you could think of was that, in the bowels of the earth, you would be safe. And the Bank tube station was the nearest to us. I went there with the baby. When I got there the platforms were crowded, there was absolutely no room. So I sat on stone stairs. It must have been about two o'clock in the morning, a man came up, probably stretching his legs or getting a breath of fresh air and he said, 'I can't let you sit there'. And I was amazed that he said, 'You take my place on the platform'. I was amazed to think that he would do that, and I went down and took his place. But that's the sort of thing that happened, people would do anything for each other.

People often shared the little they had, listened sympathetically to each other's problems, drank endless cups of tea together and joined in sing songs to cheer themselves up. These were small things but, when added up, they provided a support network that enabled people to cope with the initial shock of the bombings and shelter life.

Alongside this community spirit there grew an embryonic form of shelter organization. In a few shelters committees were democratically elected to try to improve the squalid conditions. They introduced daily cleaning rotas, regularly emptied lavatory buckets and controlled the flow of people in and out by issuing tickets. One huge, stinking cellar in Stepney which nightly housed 10,000 in conditions of appalling discomfort and overcrowding, was improved in this way by the remarkable efforts of Mickey Davis, a hunchback only just over three feet in height. The shelter, later dubbed 'Mickey's Shelter', quickly became famous for a spirit of self-help and democracy, and Mickey became a local celebrity. However there was a limit to the changes that could be made by a committee with practically no money or political influence. Substantial improvements, such as the provision of canteens, bunks and decent toilets, were dependent on assistance from local and central government – aid for which the shelter committees began to campaign strongly.

Meanwhile, Hitler was becoming more indecisive about the invasion. He put the invasion date back from 15 to 21 September hoping to buy time in which to deliver a knockout blow to the morale of London and to the R.A.F., both of which were holding up better than expected. After making this decision he launched, on 15 September, a massive air attack on London to prepare the way for the delayed invasion. The R.A.F. put every available plane into the air and won a famous victory – now annually celebrated as Battle of Britain Day. The R.A.F. destroyed around fifty German planes while sustaining losses of only about half that number. Londoners, watching the Luftwaffe's humiliation in the sky above them, were given their greatest morale booster to date. The Ministry of Information added to the euphoria by unintentionally – but not unwillingly – exaggerating the number of German planes destroyed, claiming 185 shot down, a figure eagerly seized upon by the radio and press.

Hitler's response was an intensification of the major offensive against the capital. And in this next wave of air attacks a new terror weapon was deployed. It was a huge naval mine with considerable blast effect, which fell slowly and silently on to its target by parachute. The blast from a 'land mine', as it was called, could blow a man a quarter of a mile and toss railway carriages into the air like broken toys. Yet as the attack escalated, Londoners were at least spared the horror of gas warfare, principally because Germany had little rubber which was crucial for the mass production of gas masks: she was thus vunerable to reprisals.

The redoubling of Hitler's efforts to bomb London into submission coincided with an awareness in official circles of the re-emergence of an old and potentially damaging social problem in the capital: class resentment. During the first week of bombing the East End and dockland areas were severely hit while many well-to-do parts of London were little affected. This was becoming a cause of a great deal of potentially divisive anger and hostility. In addition, working-class people heard about or saw the high life of the hotels and clubs and restaurants thriving in the West End despite the bombings. They knew about the luxurious deep shelters underneath the hotels and exclusive department stores which offered

Londoners stretch out on hammocks strung across the tracks at the Elephant and Castle tube station, early October 1940. News of luxury shelters in the West End aroused deep feelings of resentment in the tubes

night-time accommodation to wealthy clients, but which often refused to take in the East End poor who migrated west searching for a safe refuge from the bombs. Their anger was heightened by rich youths who would amuse themselves at night by 'slumming' around the tube shelters sniggering at the awful sights and smells. Emily Eary remembers the feeling of being looked down upon:

In the evenings you'd get ladies and gentlemen going home after the theatre and night-club people. And you felt they were staring and sneering at you, as much to say, 'Look at them'. You'd be there on the platform, putting your curlers in or whatever and you felt a bit humiliated. Really it was degrading because they gave the impression they were looking down on us. In fact, we were a bit resentful about it, what with them going back to their safe areas and their comfortable homes. They didn't have to go through what we did.

Car owners would frequently sail past long queues of workers – even civil defence workers – and refuse to take any passengers. Those involved in actively defending and saving the capital became particularly irritated by better-off citizens who were carrying on their lives as before. One typical example of the kind of behaviour that angered the civil defence workers occurred when a group of firemen, resting after a night-long battle against the flames, were shouted at and abused for laziness by a passing party of night-club revellers. Home Intelligence reports noted an escalation of 'class feeling' based on a popular resentment that the sacrifices of the war were being born unfairly and unequally.

The authorities were aware that this sort of class conflict could seriously undermine Londoners' will to resist. The feeling of resentment did not end even when a lone German raider attacked Buckingham Palace on 13 September. Newspapers and newsreels made much of the fact that everyone from the greatest to the lowliest was in a sense, on an equal footing in the civilian front line. Queen Elizabeth was widely quoted as saying, 'I'm glad we've been bombed. It makes me feel I can look the East End in the face.' But a few days later M.P. Harold Nicolson noted in his diary that there was still much bitterness in the East End and that the King and Queen had been booed when they visited the destroyed areas. At about this time a hundred East Enders, under Communist leadership, rushed the Savoy Hotel demanding that they be allowed to use the hotel's shelter. The unexpected sounding of the all-clear saved the management from an embarrassing situation.

Paradoxically, it was the change in German bombing strategy which generated a greater sense of unity in the capital. During the next weeks of bombing, rich and upper-class areas like Belgravia and Kensington in inner western London were hit far more frequently and heavily. So were suburban areas to the south and east, like Croydon, Wandsworth, Plumstead and Ilford. Now all Londoners, wherever they lived, had to face the terror of the blitz. And the sense of shared suffering helped to promote a new sense of cooperation and comradeship.

The first sign of this new spirit was the appearance of thousands of hitchhikers – many of them city clerks and secretaries – thumbling lifts to and from work. With many rail and bus services disrupted by the bombings, hitchhiking, which had previously been frowned upon, became the proper and patriotic thing to do. Motorists, who had earlier refused lifts, began to ferry around hitchhikers who quickly developed thumbing into a fine art by holding up destination boards and wearing badges with slogans like 'I want to go to Pimlico' and 'Say Old Bean, I'm Golders Green', or even the slightly more risqué 'Say, boys, I'm sweet, what about a seat?'

At a local level too, a new spirit of cooperation was emerging. In middle-class areas, which had previously enjoyed a reputation for stand-offishness and snobbery, neighbours found they were now dependent on one another for their survival. In places like Edgware and Carshalton the residents formed rotas for voluntary street fire-watching duties. They kitted themselves out with stirrup pumps, sandbags and pails of water to put out the incendiary bombs. Notice boards displaying street rotas sprouted in front gardens, while in back gardens housewives improvised field kitchens to cook for bombed-out families. W.V.S. volunteers collected food and blankets for the needy, secretaries and clerks doubled as fire-watchers, and families helped to clear the debris of the previous night's raid.

The new spirit of community and unified resistance mushrooming all over London often revolved around the air raid warden, who took on the position of being the leader and adviser to the neighbourhood. Quite apart from their emergency and rescue work, wardens provided information and support, guiding the people in their unit through the new jungle of war bureaucracy that was springing up: how to claim for war-damaged property, where to go to get new ration books; what were the latest evacuation and rest-centre arrangements. The good warden – and there were hundreds – inspired confidence and was of immense value in the struggle for survival.

The Lea Hall Road Firebomb Fighters, Leyton, display their primitive equipment, which includes a child's go-cart, garden tools and a dustbin lid. A new spirit of community quickly developed in suburban areas during the blitz as neighbours volunteered to do their bit

Yet, despite this growing sense of community solidarity throughout London, the suburban way of coping with the bombing remained more private than the working-class mode which developed in inner London. Whereas many East Enders packed into public shelters and entered into a

communal lifestyle, suburban families still preferred to keep themselves to themselves. They sheltered either in a safe part of the house – such as a basement strengthened against collapse by wooden 'pit props' – or in the family's Anderson in the back garden. Some of the better-off families even had specially-built garden shelters which, though still cramped, were more comfortable than the Anderson.

The blitz was often as a consequence a less traumatic experience for suburban families than for those living in places like Stepney and Bermondsey. The family's evening routine carried on much as before, though parents and children might find themselves reading books and listening to the wireless in a cramped shelter rather than in the living room. Each night Phil Barratt and his family would go to the shelter in the back garden of their house in Carshalton in Surrey:

> We had a very happy little atmosphere in our shelter. My father had it specially built just before the war and it was quite spacious. We had a little cooker, electric light, all the necessities of life. And life went on very much as usual. We had books, we had a little Pifco toaster which gave us the chance of doing a bit of toast and dripping if we felt a bit peckish in the night. There was a supply of water as well.

These feelings of a continuing element of normality were enhanced by the fact that suburban houses, by virtue of their low density layout, were far less prone to direct hits and mass destruction than the packed streets and tenements in the central areas of the city.

But whatever the difference between lifestyles, after two or three weeks people all over London were adapting themselves more easily to the blitz. In the first few days of bombing air raid warnings had created chaos: buses drew up and unloaded their passengers into the nearest shelter; post offices and shops had shut; and some older people went into a state of near panic. But by the end of September most Londoners carried on casually with whatever they were doing when the sirens went. To carry on one's normal routine uninterrupted even began to acquire a glamour. The pride and sense of purpose was particularly strong in people who had experienced some sort of near miss – preferably not too near. After an initial feeling of shock, they would chatter and joke about the experience, and come out of it feeling more important than before. In self-defence some people wore badges declaring 'I've got a bomb story too'.

Nothing illustrates this process more clearly than the 'business as usual' attitude of shopkeepers when they suffered mild bomb damage. Remaining open became a symbol of defiance, and jokey signs like 'More open than usual' or 'Blast' were quickly displayed on shop fronts to show that spirits remained high. This was the sort of spirit celebrated in the film and press propaganda of the blitz, such as in the classic 'London Can Take It' which showed ordinary people going about their business undeterred by the bombs.

Most important, Londoners kept going to work. This was of prime importance to the war effort for, quite apart from being the administrative and communications centre of Britain, London contained hundreds of munitions factories. The disruption of production during minor daylight attacks which nevertheless triggered air raid alarms – thus sending factory workers down into their shelters – was overcome after 17 September when Churchill introduced a system of roof spotters. From then on 'look-out men' would only give the alarm when a raid was truly imminent. As a result working hours lost were more than halved. Equally important in keeping up the work drive was the astonishing resilience of London transport workers who daily traversed the bomb-cratered routes to take people to work.

Quite apart from the economic advantage of keeping London working, employment also had an immense social and psychological value in the struggle to survive the blitz. Suddenly work which before may have seemed tedious and purposeless took on a new meaning; now it provided an important contribution to London's resistance against German oppression. Len Jones found that working up to seventeen hours a day as a draughtsman in Carshalton helped him to overcome the feelings of fear and horror left by his experiences on the first night of the blitz:

> To begin with, we'd all been shocked by the raids and panicked. But after a few weeks you got used to it, you took it in your stride much more. I'd cycle to work every day, even though there might be air raid warnings and bombs falling. You sort of braved the dangers because you were angry at all the destruction you saw, the destruction of the places you loved. You had to keep going, to keep up the fight against Hitler.

There was also a tremendous solidarity in the workplace. Stoppages and strikes were unheard of during the blitz, and absenteeism was minimal, partly because people thought their work-mates would worry about

Jokey signs sprouted up all over London in late September 1940. They were an expression of the mood of resistance that was developing

them being dead if they didn't turn up each morning. Also, work was a normal, and consequently comforting, routine in a time of extraordinary disruption. The fact that people had to be somewhere and do something for eight hours each day, helped them to cope with the horror. Most did not have the time or the energy to reflect too much on the incessant raids. Their preoccupation with work provided a valuable defence against the psychological damage that fear of death might otherwise have imposed upon them.

Another factor in helping Londoners to withstand the disruption and terror of the blitz was their determination to keep enjoying everyday leisure activities. Although the black-out, night attacks, and the pressure of shelter life all meant that people went out less during the evening, after the initial shock and disruption of the bombings, many continued to go to their local cinemas, dance halls and pubs. The Granada chain offered night-long shelter and entertainment for their clients, and those who stayed could look forward to five feature films and community singing. Many brought their blankets to the last house.

On 12 October, Hitler – confronted with the continued success of the R.A.F. and the interminable resistance of Londoners to his attacks – was forced to abandon his invasion plan. He had lost the Battle for London. The blitz itself was set to continue but never again would its purpose be to open the way for the Nazi invasion of Britain. Londoners, faced with relentless bombing, did not at the time realize that they had already changed the course of the war.

Exactly how and why London pulled through this nightmarish ordeal has been the subject of much popular film and literature, which together have helped to create a myth of the blitz. The received conventional wisdom is that the bombing unleashed a surge of patriotism, revealing the tremendous courage and heroism of the British character. Everyone from the grandest duke to the lowliest maid resolved to do their duty for their country, enabling Londoners to overcome all obstacles.

However this sort of 'cleaned up' picture omits and distorts many important details, hiding the rough edges of the blitz. The moments of panic and desperation, and the fragility of morale, especially during the first days of bombing, are often forgotten. And the celebration of Londoners' patriotism hides the fact that many felt anger towards the government, and that there was widespread class resentment. In fact, acts of rebellion against authority, like the invasion of the tubes, sometimes actually helped to sustain resistance. What pulled people through most of all was a tremendous community solidarity, which sprang out of shared hardship, and a grim determination to maintain as normal a routine as possible – business as usual. This struggle for survival was greatly aided by the remarkable courage and committment to the saving of London shown by the emergency services, especially the firemen.

But however much myths of the blitz may have obscured what happened in those first weeks, it is undeniable that the refusal of Londoners to give in to the Nazi air bombardment helped force Hitler to abandon Operation Sea Lion. Though worse was to come, already, in this the first phase of the blitz, Londoners had won a kind of victory.

3
LIVING WITH THE BLITZ

In the early evening of 15 October 1940, the German night bombers set off for London. This had been their routine every night since the blitz began on 7 September. As dusk fell on the capital its citizens prepared, in their different ways, for the onslaught. The spotters on the roofs stared into the sky straining for a first sight of the planes. The wardens in their control centres waited for the word that the Luftwaffe had been seen, ready to go out into the streets and warn people to take cover. The firemen at their stations checked their damaged equipment and mentally prepared themselves to face another night fighting the flames. Suburban families left the comfort of their homes for the tiny, damp Anderson shelters buried in their back gardens. And inner Londoners huddled together in crypts, cellars, street shelters and tube stations.

When darkness descended, the bombers arrived, as regular as clockwork. But on this fateful night there was a difference. There were twice as many German planes. At 8.00 p.m., the six hundred sheltered under Balham Station in south London heard a terrific explosion directly

The Balham tube disaster, October 1940. A ruined bus lies stranded in a bomb crater in Balham High Road, immediately above the station

above. A mountain of ballast, sand and water cascaded down through a huge hole at the end of the platform. The passage to the exit had been blocked by bomb blast. The whole station was rapidly submerging under this slime. Some scrambled to safety through an emergency hatch. Others remained trapped below watching the water level rise, while the rescue service struggled to reach them. Bert Woolridge was on duty at the A.R.P. centre in Balham when the station was struck:

> As I went into the entrance hundreds of people were racing out in real panic. I got to the bottom of the stairs and the entrance to the bombed platform was blocked. All you could hear was the sound of screaming

and rushing water. We managed to get to the platform by wading along through the sludge on the track, and it was terrible. People were lying there, all dead, and there was a great pile of sludge on top of them. Lots were curled up in sleeping positions on the platform. One of them – he was the porter – had had his clothes ripped off by the bomb; he lay there naked. We put the people on stretchers and carried them away through the water. I don't think we found any survivors that night.

Sixty-four Londoners died at the Balham tube disaster in what proved one tragic incident among many that night. The effects of this night of bombing, the worst so far, were devastating. The bombs had rained down from East Ham to Fulham and from Tottenham to Lewisham. Shelters were hit in Kennington, Poplar, Southwark and Waterloo, killing and injuring many. Some nine hundred fires were started. The Fleet sewer on the western outskirts of the City of London burst, pouring its contents into the Farringdon Street area. The terror lasted from dusk until five o'clock the next morning. When dawn broke and the night raiders departed, four hundred Londoners had been killed and nearly nine hundred seriously injured. Many had been made homeless, some having lost everything they possessed. It was the worst toll since the opening days of the blitz, when people had been caught completely unprepared.

Londoners were shaken, for they had believed that they were beginning to cope better. They felt they had begun to adjust to the tremendous emotional and psychological pressures of the blitz. They had been repeatedly told, in the propaganda catch-phrase of the time, that 'London can take it'. But the sheer scale of the attack made people wonder how much longer the capital could survive under this seemingly endless and ever-increasing bombardment. More urgently, nowhere now seemed safe. Within three days, three other Underground stations – Trafalgar Square, Bounds Green and Camden Town – were also the scenes of death and injury. And serious losses of life in a number of other mass shelters, including Druid Street railway arches in Bermondsey, St Peter's crypt in Southwark and several in Stoke Newington and Stepney, bit further into people's confidence.

The top secret Home Intelligence reports on London recorded 'a lowering of morale' and reported that many people felt that 'in a few months time there will be little left of London or its people'. This growing anxiety was shared by Churchill. He instructed that a search be made for the capital's strongest buildings which could be used to house the government war machine, for he believed that 'It is probable indeed that the bombing of Whitehall and the centre of Government will be continuous until all the old or insecure buildings have been demolished.'

The cabinet could see no reason why Hitler should call off his attack. More important, neither did Hitler. Although the German High Command had by now abandoned their plan to invade Britain that autumn, they had not abandoned their faith in mass bombing. Even if Britain could not be conquered by invasion, it might nevertheless be possible to force a

St Pancras Station was one of the many victims of the escalation in bombing raids late in 1940. Many feared that all London would soon be razed to the ground

surrender by inflicting extensive devastation. The lesson the Nazi commanders drew from their failure to bring Britain to her knees was that the intensity of the bombing had been insufficient and the time-scale too short. What was needed was a stepping-up of the bombing campaign.

The Luftwaffe's attack on London was set to last. Moreover, there was nothing at the time that Britain could do about it. During the early days of the blitz, when the Luftwaffe had been making day as well as night raids, the R.A.F. had been able to destroy a considerable number of enemy planes. But now that the Luftwaffe had decided to make raids only under the cover of darkness, Fighter Command found that it was impotent. The defence of London was left to the ack ack units and, although the thunder of their guns was comforting to Londoners, only very occasionally did they chance on hitting a German plane. London was practically defenceless against the night raider. The military was giving top priority to developing an effective system of defence but, so far, air-borne radar was not yet operational. Londoners were left with living with the blitz.

As the air attacks continued relentlessly, the problem of homelessness reached crisis proportions in the bomb-ravaged capital. A host of difficulties were mounting and two became critical: the provision for those growing numbers of Londoners whose homes had been damaged or destroyed by bombing, and the conditions in the mass shelters. Without action to solve these problems, the ability of London to keep on 'taking it' was in doubt.

Each night hundreds of houses were destroyed, and many more were damaged; each night streets all over the capital were cratered, the network of pipes and mains beneath ruptured. Each morning, many were left homeless, often with all their possessions destroyed. In Stepney, one of the worst hit boroughs, about forty per cent of the houses had been damaged or destroyed by early November 1940. Thousands more found that though their home was still standing the basic services – gas, electricity, water – had been cut off. On one night, the bombings resulted in a fifth of London's households being without gas. In the first weeks of the blitz, people had resolutely put up with not being able to cook or wash

The shattered remains of Stepney Way in the East End, autumn 1940. The problem of home-lessness in the bomb-ravaged capital was reaching crisis proportions

but, by now, they were expecting greater support from the authorities. In the East End families faced these problems daily, yet often there was still nowhere they could go for a good cheap meal, or to wash themselves or their clothes. When George Golder, his mother Hannah and two sisters, Emily and Alice, were bombed out from their dockside home in Silvertown, they camped out in a brick street shelter:

> We hadn't had a proper meal for days so I went back home to try and knock something up. There was no gas or water or electricity in the house, but I managed to salvage some bacon and I made a bonfire in the back garden with some broken wood. I was in the middle of cooking the bacon when the landlord came along and asked about the rent. I told him to clear off. I had my little meal but the house was in too bad a state to try and live there again.

Gladys Strelitz was slightly more successful in feeding her family, with a do-it-yourself kitchen in the back garden of her bombed-out home in East Ham:

> We had no light you see, there was no gas, no electricity – that had been cut off – and all we could rely on was a candle. The house was a mess. Well, I found these four bricks and I put them like a diamond on the back step, and filled it up with paper, bracken and a piece of wood. I'd put the saucepan on that, and stir and make the porridge for the children. 'When will it be ready, mummy?' 'Not long now.' We would put the kettle on and have a cup of tea. We really were scouts.

Voluntary groups, like the W.V.S., the Y.M.C.A. and the Salvation Army, had struggled to provide at least some of the most basic services since the early days of the blitz. They ran mobile canteens for families unable to cook for themselves. But this army of volunteers, who were largely funded through the collection box, could not cater for people's needs en masse. They did not have enough mobile canteens and, anyway, this was only a temporary 'morning-after' solution. If your gas was cut off for days, a cup of tea and a bun served in the street was clearly inadequate. A proper public meal service was needed but that required indoor canteen facilities which the voluntary groups had neither the buildings nor the equipment to provide. Most important, those whose homes had been destroyed needed to be rehoused – and the voluntary groups simply did not have the power to do this.

The responsibility for solving this emerging crisis lay with London's local authorities. But the only real progress achieved was in tackling the food crisis. The inner London area came under the authority of the London County Council, which covered twenty-nine boroughs stretching from Hammersmith to Woolwich and Islington to Lewisham. As a large and well-resourced organization, the L.C.C. proved to be more dynamic than the individual borough councils. Working together in close cooperation, the L.C.C. provided facilities, the voluntary groups provided staff, and the Ministry of Food provided money. More mobile canteens were put on the road, though plans for a proper meals service in sit-down dining rooms were hampered by a shortage of stoves.

But the homeless also needed shelter, clothes, household goods and money. As days of going without these basic necessities turned into weeks, people became increasingly depressed or even demoralized. Emily Golder recalls:

> It was difficult to manage without being able to wash yourself or your clothes and without anywhere to go. We went to the council who bused us out to the Majestic cinema in Woodford. It was a great tall building, terribly unsafe. There were no facilities, nowhere to wash or eat. We slept in the cinema seats, you could only get a cap nap. And after a few days we were moved to St Stephen's church in Walthamstow. There was nothing there. We slept on straw on the floor. We didn't know what was going to happen next. We couldn't get to Silvertown from there and so we lost our jobs. Then we were moved again to Finchley Rest Centre. We felt like refugees.

Helping the homeless came under the Poor Law Acts which, despite reforms in the inter-war years, still maintained a rather punitive attitude towards poverty that reached back to stern Victorian values. This meant that responsibility lay with the Public Assistance Committees of the L.C.C. or with the local borough. Many of these committees held harsh Dickensian views about the treatment of needy families and all of them suffered from lack of resources. Consequently, provision tended to be meagre and parsimonious, and access to welfare hand outs was governed by the old 'mean's test'. People, who had already gone through the

devastating experience of losing everything they had, faced the bureaucratic and humiliating process of 'proving' that they were penniless. The
whole procedure was gaining the town halls an infamous reputation. The
secret Home Intelligence records carried, for example, a report from one
of their observers in Chelsea:

> Bombed people don't enjoy answering more than a certain number of
> questions and they hate being treated as criminal paupers. People
> know that Americans and Canadians have sent warm things for the
> unfortunate of Chelsea. They know that it is no easy thing to get them
> from those experienced in the tough administration of Charity who
> dole them out after the Town Hall has satisfied itself that the applicant
> is sufficiently near death from exposure. . . . This business is a scan-
> dal. People are talking about it and they don't like it. They are treated
> like rabble.

*An 85-year-old lady joins the
children queuing up for a basin of
soup at a small south-east London
rest centre in the early days of the
blitz. To begin with the rest
centres were spartan, badly
organized and provided little
support for bombed-out families*

Meanwhile, the rest centres, the converted church halls and schools
temporarily housing the homeless, continued to be totally inadequate.
Though there had been improvements from the first days of the blitz,
when these hastily improvised centres were marked by the stench of no
sanitation, there was a dire shortage of any facilities that would make
them less of an ordeal for the shell-shocked families that entered their
doors. They often remained spartan, badly organized, and unable to help
with the simplest of queries from a bombed-out family. They desperately
needed more blankets, mattresses and camp beds for sleeping, more cups
and teapots, and more chairs and tables to make people feel welcome,
even 'at home'.

These improvements were impossible under the old Poor Law with its mean provisions. A new approach which was both more generous and provided help on the basis of 'need' alone, without the mean's test, was required. There was considerable support in the coalition government, particularly among the Labour members, for such a change. Most important, Herbert Morrison, who had campaigned against the Poor Law in the pre-war years, was now, as Minister for Home Security, one of the key figures involved in the debate. And at the Ministry of Health, the other key department directly responsible, officials had become convinced of the need for change by the urgency and seriousness of the problem. However, the Treasury held out against such moves throughout October.

The crisis of homelessness was, in the meantime, steadily worsening. By mid-October, roughly 250,000 Londoners had been made homeless by the bombings. Given the lack of help from local councils, most went to stay with friends or relations. Such arrangements were, of course, far better for the homeless than having nowhere to live, but they generally resulted in serious overcrowding and did not offer a long-term solution to the problem. Len Jones and his entire family descended on his sister's maisonette in Carshalton:

> We all went to 32 Wrythe Lane to my sister's little maisonette. There were eighteen of us there in two rooms because we were all bombed out. My father fixed up scaffold boards along the walls and at night ten of us would sleep in one room, all in line, and eight in the other little room. Of course we didn't get much sleep. Outside my father fixed up some buckets for washing for the men and built a latrine. In the garden there was a bit of a grass patch and my brother-in-law fixed up a ridge tent, so I used to sleep in that with three or four of the other men.

Charlie Draper and his family had an even more tragi-comic time in his aunt's back garden in Peckam:

> Our family ended up all of us living in Aunty's Anderson shelter. We were bombed out, the house was in ruins, so Aunty let us stay with her. It was incredible inside, there was six of us but there was only room for one big bed so we all slept in it, and it was a case of one turns and you all turn. And I used to wear Wellington boots at the time and I had very smelly feet and often they wouldn't let me in until I'd taken them off or washed my feet, and the bombs would be raining down and I'd be saying 'Let me in'.

More urgent, however, was the growing army of homeless families who had no choice but to go to the overcrowded rest centres. This dispossessed population was largest in the L.C.C. area where the damage to housing was most extensive. Although new centres were opened by the Council, the great mass of people sleeping in them meant that conditions were becoming intolerable.

The homeless families needed to be rehoused. But this was largely the responsibility of the individual borough councils and not the larger

L.C.C. – and so far many of these smaller councils had been quite unable to meet the new challenges thrown up by the blitz. During the first six weeks of the blitz, the councils in the London region had rehoused only a little over 7,000 of the 250,000 homeless in the capital.

The problem in this area was primarily one of organizational failure. Although some progressive councils like Bermondsey and Lambeth had in the inter-war years developed mini welfare states in their boroughs, many others were run by an 'old guard' of councillors and officials who were set in their ways and who jealously guarded their power. They would carry on with the old bureaucratic and penny-pinching ways of doing things – ways which even in the pre-war years were often inefficient. Now they were disastrous. Many of the councillors, Labour as well as Tory, were suspicious of new ideas, especially if they had any connection with the Communist Party, which was crusading for sweeping changes in government provision. In fact, dealing with the lack of accommodation for the homeless did require a radical approach, challenging in particular the sanctity of private ownership of property. For there was a glut of empty houses in London at this time and the councils had the power to requisition these properties and then use them as billets for homeless families. Yet they were not using this power, despite the dire problems the homeless faced. In one local authority, left unidentified in the official records, the council's chief billeting officer was also the local estate agent, who looked after his own business interests to such an extent that not one property had been requisitioned by the end of October.

Ministry of Health reports repeatedly emphasized the slowness of requisitioning in London:

> In one borough which is full of empty houses only three have been requisitioned and got ready in a week, another was still relying on voluntary billeting on householders, another had on a certain day eight hundred people needing billeting and only six vacancies available. There appeared to be a universal shortage of billeting officers, the work of finding billets being left to the Women's Voluntary Service.

What made matters worse was that the most inefficient boroughs were also often the worst hit. The people of Stepney, for example, faced not only the heaviest air attacks but also a borough council which, according to government inspectors, was in 'unbelievable chaos' with no billeting or rehousing departments despite two months of bombing.

The crisis in many London boroughs was by now so deep that the war cabinet discussed taking away the responsibility for rehousing from local councils and handing it to a special commissioner for London, a sort of 'London dictator'. They decided against it partly because the government's own attempts to alleviate homelessness were equally unsuccessful. The Ministry of Health, for example, organized through local councils the transfer of several thousand East Enders into empty houses in well-to-do western and north-western boroughs like Paddington, Hampstead, Finchley and Westminster. But the newcomers, many of whom were poor, complained of the extra travelling costs to work and the lack of cheap shops locally. The families, already feeling stressed from being bombed out, also found these strange settings, with their more formal conventions, a terrible strain. They missed the warmth of the tightly-knit communities from which they had seldom strayed before the war. And they felt in limbo without their basic home comforts and conveniences. Alice Golder and her family were eventually billeted in Finchley:

When we arrived we all looked a bit dirty and dishevelled and the lady of the house decided that she didn't want us in and she wouldn't open the door. The billeting officer said 'You've got to open the door by law and let them in' and eventually she did. We felt awful. We were put in the attic, there were two rooms. Me and my sister had to share a bed with mum and my brothers went in the other room. There was nowhere to cook and the lady wouldn't let us bring food in the house. She didn't like us in the house in day-time and so we spent most of the day in the park. We'd eat some sandwiches, sit on benches or walk around to keep warm. We would have gone back to the East End if we could, but our home was totally uninhabitable.

Many East Enders did drift back home to bombed-out Bermondsey, Poplar and Stepney. The scheme was quickly wound down.

The government also attempted to alleviate the crisis of homelessness in London by extending their evacuation scheme, which had been hastily restarted for children after the first heavy raids back in September. Mothers and their children from anywhere in London were now entitled to a place. And the scheme did meet with some success. Though in the early weeks of the blitz people had shown little interest in evacuation, wanting in part to make a resolute stand against Hitler, by this stage the acute housing problems of many families and the relentlessness of the bombing meant that more and more chose to leave the capital. Amongst them was Gladys Strelitz and her children:

We couldn't live a life like that much longer there was still no light, no gas no electricity, it's been cut off, and we were living in draughts and cold. We had to put all our blankets round the windows to keep out the draughts. And all the children were running round in the debris and I was trying to cook in the back garden. It was all so much of a worry that in the end we had to do something about it so we decided there and then that we'd go to Reading.

In October, 89,000 mothers and children were evacuated under the official scheme. Though this was far fewer than the three-quarters of a million mothers and children who had been evacuated at the outset of war – many of whom were now back in London – the scheme was making some impact on the housing crisis.

But, like the first evacuation, this exodus into the provinces turned sour once the London families reached their destination. The bombed-out families were usually dirty, bedraggled and surprised to be treated with

Evacuees on their way to billets in the countryside pass a detachment of troops at Waterloo Station. In October 1940, 89,000 mothers and children were officially evacuated, an exodus which helped to relieve the housing crisis a little

contempt by some of the reception families. As censorship meant that few people outside London realized the devastating impact of the blitz, many in the reception areas did not appreciate the appalling conditions from which the evacuees were escaping. In addition, numerous day-to-day difficulties arose. Though the reception families were often better off than the evacuees, they were not wealthy. They usually had little or no spare space. The evacuated families might end up sleeping four or five to a bed. There was at the same time little or no help from the local councils in the reception areas with washing or cooking facilities. The end result was tension and friction between the London evacuees and the local residents. By the beginning of November 1940 the numbers leaving London were reduced to a trickle.

This all meant that the problem of rehousing the homeless was left primarily to the individual borough councils. But the councils were by now sinking into deeper difficulties. As well as failing to requisition empty houses, they were falling way behind with repairs to bomb-damaged property.

Families, who could have returned to their own homes if fairly minor repairs had been done, instead joined the army of homeless. At the same time the stock of houses available for repairs continued to shrink. To some extent the problem of repairs stemmed from the sheer immensity of the damage. But it was also brought about by the bumbledom and inaction of some councils. Stepney, for example, refused to employ outside contractors, even though its own labour force was completely swamped with work.

Moreover, the crisis was aggravating overcrowding in the shelters. With nowhere else to go, many of the homeless simply set up home in the shelters. More and more homeless East End families went down to the Chislehurst caves in Kent, which by the end of October were housing around 15,000 people.

The cave-dwellers had to make the best of the primitive conditions. The caves were cold and dim, lit only by candlelight. There were no washing or toilet facilities; the cave-dwellers had to walk a mile or more to relieve themselves outside. In the first days of the blitz, some families had tried to make it a real home by bringing beds, armchairs and sideboards with them. But as the caves became more and more overcrowded people were jam packed together sleeping on the rough floors. And even then, on some nights there might be hundreds left in the open air outside, unable to get in.

Similarly, squalor and overcrowding in the mass shelters in inner London was worsening. By now, some 350,000 were taking refuge in public shelters each night. Some of the worst conditions were in the tubes where scabies, impetigo and lice were increasing at an alarming rate. The Eary family were sheltering in the Underground at Moorgate. Emily recalls the awful health risks there:

> The sanitary arrangements were appalling. There were still no proper toilets on the station, only chemical latrines, and they were so inadequate they overflowed all the time. There was nowhere to wash and you might be sleeping next to sick people. My brother Ernest got enteritis. And we all went down with scabies. We had to go to a rescue unit and they slapped disinfectant all over us with a big paint brush. It was horrible. We had the treatment three times. Then they baked all our clothes.

And, as winter set in, so too did the cold-weather ailments of flu', colds and bronchitis. There was concern that this ill-health was weakening people's resistance and making them vulnerable to the spread of more serious diseases like tuberculosis. The prospect of an epidemic loomed ever larger.

As the difficulties mounted and as the shelterers themselves became more weary, the limited improvements gained by the shelterers co-operating together began to be threatened. In th early days of the blitz a community spirit had flowered on the tube platforms and grimy shelter floors which had helped the people pull through. But as overcrowding and conditions worsened, competition and bitter rivalry for the 'best' places emerged. When people saw their own immediate safety and health, and even their lives, as being dependent on fighting for themselves and their family, then community and co-operation took second place. Emily Eary recalls this frightening shift in attitudes:

> It was a real survival of the fittest. You'd queue for hours to get a good spot on the platform – you'd want to avoid the cold, draughty and smelly parts. People would spread newspapers on the floor or leave bundles to show it was their territory and somebody might come and kick them away and that would lead to arguments over who should be where. Sometimes you'd get people squaring up and fights. Mum was like a hen fighting for her brood.

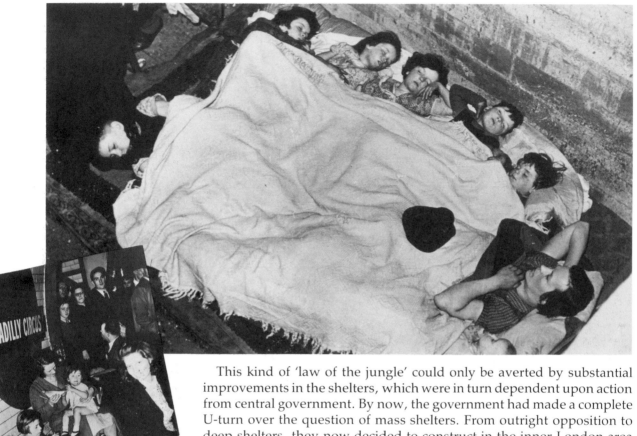

Some of the worst conditions for shelterers were in the overcrowded tubes like Piccadilly (inset). Scabies, impetigo and lice increased at an alarming rate amongst families camping out on the platforms. Top: A mother and her children snuggle up under a blanket underneath the Bermondsey railway arches

This kind of 'law of the jungle' could only be averted by substantial improvements in the shelters, which were in turn dependent upon action from central government. By now, the government had made a complete U-turn over the question of mass shelters. From outright opposition to deep shelters, they now decided to construct in the inner London area eight enormous purpose-built underground shelters, each holding 8,000 people. Herbert Morrison, who persuaded his cabinet colleagues of the need to divert scarce building resources to this enterprise, argued that the plan was essential to counter Communist agitation on the deep shelter issue, which was striking an increasingly popular chord.

At the same time, the government set about replacing the outdoor Anderson with an indoor home shelter; partly so that those who did not have a garden could shelter at home and thereby relieve the pressure on the public shelters; though partly also because life for those with an Anderson was becoming increasingly unpleasant as the cold and damp of winter set in. Eventually, the new shelter named after the Minister, the 'Morrison' – a steel-framed box which could be used as a table in day-time – was designed but its mass production was months away.

Until the distant day when these new developments would come to fruition, those without an Anderson or any safe place to shelter at home had to make do with the existing mass shelters. Often these structures were quite unsuitable and totally ill-equipped for housing hundreds, even thousands, of families. Places like the railway arches in Bermondsey were dank, with water streaming down the walls. Many, like the notorious Tilbury shelter in Stepney where 12,000 regularly took refuge, were not connected to the sewage system. Little could be done about the stench

and the accumulation of excrement, for proper sanitation required major excavations. Most lacked any heating or ventilation and were consequently at different times bitingly cold or swelteringly hot. The shelters provided by the government prior to the blitz were turning out to be equally unsatisfactory. The surface brick shelters were seen – with some justification – as unsafe. And the 'trench' shelters, which were dug a few feet into the ground, were damp underfoot and increasingly prone to leak through the roof.

Even when improvements were possible, by providing, for example, bunks or first-aid posts, they were painfully slow in coming. The government readily handed out instructions to shelterers on how to keep their shelter in order through cleaning up their own patch, putting their blankets away, or not sleeping in the pathways, but practical help was less forthcoming.

The shelterers were becoming increasingly disillusioned with the authorities. Home Intelligence was carefully monitoring the discontent through reports from its observers. They noted the shelterers' response to government instructions on keeping the shelter in good order: 'The experienced dwellers of the shelters realized that these were obviously the work of those with no knowledge of life underground. The notes were laughed at and produced a bitter cynicism which is becoming more and more evident of late.'

Far left: *Latrines overflow onto the floor of an air raid shelter in Stoke Newington, while in a trench shelter (above), children are tied to the bench to prevent them falling onto the flooded floor. This was the grim reality of sheltering for many thousands of Londoners, though it was hushed up in the press*

The authorities, on the other hand, were often extremely suspicious of the shelterers, especially those who agitated for improvements. The loudest voices demanding change were often those of the Communists, but they tended to be dismissed by the government as 'subversives' even though the reforms they advocated were practical and moderate, and often had widespread support among the shelterers. The authorities were also often distrustful of the elected committees which were also seen as the work of 'agitators'. Nina Hibbin recalls an incident at the Tilbury shelter which illustrates dramatically this deep antagonism:

> People had started to organize but of course there was a limit to what ordinary people could do. I mean they could club together and buy first-aid equipment, they could bring their own folding stools, they could allocate places or make sure that the older people had a decent place but they couldn't pump out the wet. There was so much wet on the floor, sometimes you were actually wading in it. They couldn't provide the latrines because obviously that's a professional job, so it was only the authorities, the A.R.P. or the town hall authorities who could make any really substantial improvements. The people were so angry that they decided to take a deputation to the A.R.P. There already was a rudimentary shelter committee and the people who were on it got together and went to the A.R.P. headquarters with certain demands like decent sanitation, bunks with proper tickets and bunk allocation – that kind of thing, very simple things. Well when they got to the A.R.P., there were about forty of us. I went along with them. All of a sudden we find that we're being charged by mounted police. They came pouring through the entrance wielding their batons, and I remember one of them got hold of a man with a bandage round his neck and began beating him up. And then a number of people were taken to the police station, and that was the end of our delegation.

The violence of this response was unusual, probably reflecting the officials' fears that the Tilbury, based as it was in the Communist Party stronghold of Stepney, was a hotbed of revolution. But even when the requests for improvements could not be dismissed as simply 'Communist-inspired', they met with little success. For example, the committees representing the shelterers in Swiss Cottage Underground – who were professional middle-class people – found that their requests for proper medical care were passed constantly between the Health Ministry, the local authority and London Transport. And while the authorities dallied, a child died of meningitis. The Swiss Cottage shelterers, who saw themselves as a very moderate group, were incensed. In the *Swiss Cottager*, their own unique station newspaper that they managed to print, they complained 'against shameful apathy, indifference amounting almost to callousness, neglect, soulless contempt for elementary human decencies, against red tape, authority, and officialdom, and against practised experts in the time-honoured game of "passed-to-you-please".'

By early November, the government was facing an increasingly angry and disillusioned population in the blitzed capital. Whether in the nightly routine of shelter life or in the desperate plight of being bombed out, people bitterly felt that their lives were made more difficult by official inaction. The war cabinet's civil defence committee had been told that it was becoming difficult to restrain the press from criticism, despite the fact that censorship, often self-imposed, had meant that until now there had been almost total silence on all these problems. Morale, the country's leaders were warned, would be seriously undermined if action was not taken.

Then, unexpectedly, the pressure on London was lifted. On the night of 14 November there was a clear sky, but for the first time since 7 September the Luftwaffe did not take the opportunity of bombing the capital. For on that night they instead blitzed Coventry, leaving behind them a devastated city. The Luftwaffe's changed tactics meant that the consecutive nights of bombing in the capital had come to an end. For sixty-seven successive nights – with one exception in early November when bad weather had kept the Luftwaffe away – the capital had faced death and destruction. Now it shared the burden of air attacks with the other major industrial centres of Britain as Germany stepped up its bombing campaign. London was still to suffer more raids and more bombs than any other city, but the problems stemming from the sheer continuity of the attack on the capital had gone. For, though the bombers did return for three more consecutive nights, in the next month there were only three raids on London.

London had a breathing space. This was a great opportunity to try to overcome the crises stemming from the destruction of the capital. Repairs to houses could be tackled without the depressing prospect of knowing that there would be even more by the next day. But for there to be substantial progress there had to be a change of heart in official circles.

First, the old-fashioned Poor Law attitudes which treated the victims of bombing damage as paupers had to be swept away. Those, like Morrison, who had argued from the early days of the blitz for an emphasis on people's needs, first and foremost, now began to win the day. At the end of November, the Treasury, which had previously resisted this change, caved in and agreed to finance all the costs of sorting out the problems of the homeless. From now on, a new emphasis on welfare was to be the mark of the authorities' approach to the blitz victims. The needs of ordinary Londoners took on a significance they had not had in the pre-war years. They had suffered a great deal through the blitz and the government was concerned that their morale should not crack. Their continuing support was essential for the war effort and turning a blind eye to their problems was planting dangerous seeds of discontent. There was a new consensus that in this, the 'people's war', the people's needs had to be met, or, at least, had to be seen to be taken seriously.

Secondly, the whole system of tackling the crisis created by the blitz had to become more efficient. The bureaucratic muddles of the local councils, their inaction and their parochial attitudes had to go. There was a slow but steady move towards greater central government control and intervention. Increasingly, people felt that the ultimate responsibility for tackling the problems lay with the state. The war cabinet, in particular, had the power to determine how the nation's effort and resources were used. They could, for example, divert labour and equipment from industry and the armed services into assisting the blitzed capital. The state was set to become an increasingly important influence on people's everyday lives.

With both these sets of changes underway, improvements began at last to materialize. The government called in the Army to help out with repairs in the most hard-pressed boroughs. Though the standards were very low – usually just a rough patching to protect against wind and weather – a start could be made on returning the homeless to their own houses.

To help Londoners through these difficult times, support was increasingly provided for jobs once seen as the responsibility of the housewife. Dirty clothes, for example, could be taken to a mobile 'washing van' which would do the laundry for free. Meals could be eaten out in one of the new public canteens that were springing up as a result of army stoves being requisitioned for the kitchens. In inner London in particular, the L.C.C. was quick to take advantage of Ministry of Food funds and soon one of these new 'communal feeding centres' was being opened up virtually every day. Within three months, the L.C.C. Londoners' Meals Service had opened 104 restaurants, serving 10,000 meals a day. In the East End there was eventually one about every half mile. The meals at these communal canteens – or 'British Restaurants' as they later became known – were nutritious and extremely cheap, costing about 10d. to one shilling a head and were rapidly extended to unbombed areas to supplement scanty rations.

By helping more people to live at home, the authorities eased the pressure on the rest centres. Overcrowding was reduced. At the same time, adequate sleeping facilities, toilets and dining rooms serving hot meals began to be provided. In addition, all the council services required by the homeless began to be there under one roof. While the children were looked after in the crèche, the parents could go to the rehousing officer to sort out billeting arrangements, make a request for furniture or household equipment, and meet a council official who would help them with cash or ration books. There would be an advice centre, often run by the W.V.S., to pick up any other problems. While the red tape had not disappeared altogether, it was at least easier to cope with than in the early months of the blitz, when the homeless often found they had to walk as many as eight miles to get round all the council departments that needed to be visited.

At the same time, central government started to take greater control over local billeting procedures. Each council was instructed to appoint officers who had to ensure that billets were found. All the properties in the borough had to be surveyed regularly to see where there was spare capacity. Empty properties had to be requisitioned as necessary and made ready for immediate occupation. Furniture was to be provided, though the short supply meant that this was often very minimal. Once a family had been billeted or rehoused, they would be visited by a welfare officer to see what difficulties the move was creating. The emphasis throughout was on trying to meet the particular needs of each individual family. Emily Golder and her family were eventually rehoused in a semi-detached house in Hendon Lane, Finchley:

> To begin with it was very primitive. There was no heating and no furniture, and we had to sleep on the floorboards. But bit by bit, things got better. You got a welfare officer coming round and sorting things out and the council set us up with our cooker and made sure that we had water and bedding and everything we needed. And when the neighbours got to hear about us they were very nice, and they'd offer us furniture and things. And because we were settled we'd all been able to get jobs in the area and start earning again. We felt we were beginning to live again, we were really thankful for what was done for us.

Solving the problem of homelessness would take time, and in particular those crowded in with relations would be there a lot longer, but at last the crisis was being tackled, efficiently and with compassion.

In some of the shelters, too, conditions were slowly getting better. Structural improvements were undertaken to overcome the problems of damp, sanitation and ventilation. As a result, major epidemics were avoided. In Chislehurst, the local district council and central government stepped in to improve the conditions and safety of the vast sub-terranean community of shelterers, camped in the caves. They introduced electric lighting, improved sanitation and flattened the floors. In other shelters, in particular the Underground, basic facilities, such as first-aid posts and bunks, also began to be provided. Some tube trains were converted into 'refreshment specials', moving from station to station serving tea and cocoa, sausage rolls and pies, cakes and buns. Sometimes entertainment would be organized with E.N.S.A. performers or even top-ranking artists like George Formby.

But the problems were so extensive and time so short that many shelters were left untouched throughout November. At the end of the month, a tube shelterers' conference was held – organized by the shelter committees from Swiss Cottage, King's Cross, Euston, Old Street, Moorgate, Tottenham Court Road and Hampstead – to press for a speedier rate of improvement. For these shelterers, as for those in other mass shelters, it seemed that they were waiting too long. The Home Intelligence reports monitored continuing discontent. In early December, the report on the East End noted: 'There are many shelters that are still dripping with water and lack proper sanitation, drainage and ventilation. The people habitually using these shelters have a sense of grievance. . . . They have had official visits and seen many promises in the press of improvements – but improvement does not materialize. Bitterness and apathy grow.'

There had been progress – but it was too slow. Nowhere was this was more evident than in the fire service. For while Londoners had benefitted from the lull in the bombing of the capital, the London Fire Brigade had not. They had been rushing around the country helping out the desperately undermanned and ill-equipped services of the provincial towns and

A display of requisitioned taxis doubling up as fire engines, complete with white-painted mudguards and runnerboards to aid visibility during the blackout. This was the sort of Heath Robinson-style equipment the auxiliary fire brigade had to contend with in the early days of the blitz

cities. Since the first days of the blitz they had been hindered by a lack of modern equipment like turntable ladders, heat-resistant hosing, fire engines, and so on. Though some extra equipment had arrived during the lull, the problems remained much as they had been two months earlier. The German bombings, however, were becoming increasingly better planned for maximum fire damage. London's next warning of the dangers came on 8 December when the Luftwaffe dropped over three thousand incendiary bombs, eight times more than on the first day of the blitz.

Then, just a few days after Christmas, came the greatest challenge so far for London's fire service. On the night of 29 December the Germans bombed the City of London. The Luftwaffe dropped hundreds of incendiary cannisters on the comercial heart of the capital when no one was on watch. Businessmen had gone home for the night, double-locking their property behind them. Banks, offices, churches and houses rapidly caught alight and the flames spread like a forest fire through the narrow streets.

It was now that the price was to be paid for the flaws in London's fire service. As the fires began to rage through the City, the firemen found that the water in their hoses turned to a trickle. The mains in the area had been hit and their back-up systems from distant pipes failed. They turned to the Thames for help, and struggled across the mud to extract the river water. But that night it was an exceptionally low tide. The water could not be reached.

The fires spread into a massive conflagration which raged uncontrollably across the heart of London, consuming its oldest and most historic area, the City of London itself. From the roof of St Paul's Cathedral, the fire-fighters could look down on a carpet of fire stretching into the distance – and do nothing. But eventually, the tide in the Thames turned, water came back to the hoses and the fires were controlled.

By then the damage had been done. The inferno had reduced great swathes of the City of London to charred rubble in what was one of the worst nights of destruction of the whole war. In the Barbican and Moorgate areas almost every building was ruined. On the South Bank – to which the fires had spread – a strip of houses and warehouses a mile long and a quarter of a mile wide was destroyed. The streets around St Paul's were now blackened shells, though the Cathedral itself had been saved, partly as a result of more vigilant fire-watching followed by swift preventive action. For many Londoners going to work the next morning, St Paul's symbolized a renewed defiance in the face of the enemy's onslaught as it stood majestically above the smouldering ruins.

A still from a war office cine-film shot from St Paul's Cathedral, with Paternoster Row in flames, 29 December 1940. Below: Firemen tackle flames during the great fire. After a few hours, the water in their hoses ran dry and the fire spread uncontrollably. Great swathes of the City of London were reduced to rubble

The events of that fateful night added a sense of urgency to the fight against the bombing. The very next day, new fire-watching laws were brought in to ensure that no property was left unguarded. Men between the ages of sixteen and sixty had to register for compulsory fire-watching forty-eight hours a month. New equipment was ordered to tackle the shortage of water during raids. But many of the men fighting the fire felt that, perhaps, the most important problem – the lack of cooperation and coordination between local fire services – had been ignored. For the fire service was saddled with a remarkably bureaucratic structure: local councils ruled that their fire brigades should only fire calls in their own borough; they were not allowed to provide assistance to other areas, even though they might not be using their men and equipment while other parts of London were burning down. It was the London Fire Brigade together with the newly created auxiliary firemen, under the control of the Minister for Home Security, who had fought the raging fires in central London.

On 31 December after nearly forty-eight hours of fighting the fires, Charlie Chambers returned to his station at Dagenham: 'Well we were fed up, tired, weary, eyes bloodshot and when I got back to the station and saw all the equipment there and I thought, "God, you know". Oh, I saw some of the boys and they said "What was it like" and I said "Bloody awful". So they said "You're lucky, we're not allowed out". I said "We're not lucky mate, you're the lucky ones, not us".'

The government, however, was still reluctant to take control of the fire service. Morrison, in particular, saw it as the 'brightest jewel in the local authorities' crown' and was afraid of offending the local councils by taking it away from them.

And the problems of the shelters, too, continued to dog the government. On 5 January 1941, the L.C.C. member Lord Cranley described in the *Sunday Times* a tour of the shelters in the London area. 'I was implored', he stated, 'to do anything that was possible to alleviate their appalling conditions.' In early January, the heavy raids continued, causing much devastation and many a tragedy. The Bank tube station, for example, received a direct hit and 111 shelterers died. Morale was sinking to a new low.

The discontent came to a head on 12 January when the Communist Party organized a 'People's Convention' in central London. Over two thousand 'delegates' met to call for a 'people's peace'. The feeling, concluded the Mass Observer present, was that people were 'looking for a way out of the present mess'. Though the claim that these 'delegates' represented over a million people was no doubt exaggerated, the numbers involved were large enough to worry the government. A week later, Morrison banned the Communists' paper, *The Daily Worker*, which had been in the forefront of the campaign to improve conditions for shelterers and bombed-out families.

The government realized, however, that repression was a dangerous, and possibly counter-productive, way of dealing with people's discontent and that to maintain morale the remaining problems created by the blitz had to be tackled yet more urgently. The authorities were helped out by another lull in the attacks. In February, the weather was exceptionally bad and there were few raids on London for a month. There was a renewed chance for substantial improvements.

In the fire service, new equipment started to arrive. There was even time for training sessions in its use. New water mains began to be laid on the surface which, unlike the mains underground, did not shatter when a bomb fell in the area, because of their greater flexibility. In the spring, Herbert Morrison, under pressure from the fire chiefs, finally accepted the need to 'nationalize' the fire service and form one fire-fighting body called the National Fire Service, though this was not in operation until the summer.

During this period, the crisis in the shelters was also finally tackled. Basic facilities became widely available, with 22,000 bunkbeds, for

Shelterers enjoying the 'luxury' of bunk beds at the Elephant and Castle tube station. Improvements in sheltering conditions in the later stages of the blitz made possible the flowering of a lasting community spirit underground

example, being installed in the Underground. Shelterers in the tubes would now be allocated a ticket for a specific bunk that was theirs, as long as they slept there regularly. The physical improvements and the better organization ended the battles for the 'best' places and a feeling of neighbourliness began again to develop. It was at this stage, much more than in the early and more desperate days of the blitz, that a deep and lasting 'community spirit' really flourished. Rene Eary recalls:

> You got a real community going after it was organized better. Until then everyone had been shifting around and you didn't hardly know anyone. But now you had a regular spot with the same bunks every night, and the people around you became like regular neighbours. We'd play with the kids next door so to speak, and everyone would be gossiping and playing cards with each other. It was a settled community.

In the Chislehurst caves the combined efforts of the owner, Mr Gardiner, the government and the shelterers had created a remarkable community life deep underground in which bunk beds, canteens, a children's chapel and a cave hospital were some of the amenities provided. When Charlie Draper joined his grandmother to live in the caves in spring 1941 the level of organization was quite astonishing:

> When I first came down the caves, I was amazed; it was like a city under ground. I found my gran, and she saved me a bunk. They had two-tier bunks, and they were a luxury then. So I put my blanket and my pillow out, and put my tools under the bed, and I said I'm going to have a roam round. I went a few caves up and found there was a dance hall,

A Salvation Army band entertain the shelterers in the Chislehurst caves, Kent. By the spring of 1941 the caves had been transformed into a remarkable underground city, offering the 12,000 or so regular shelterers a great array of services, including canteens, a cave hospital and a cinema

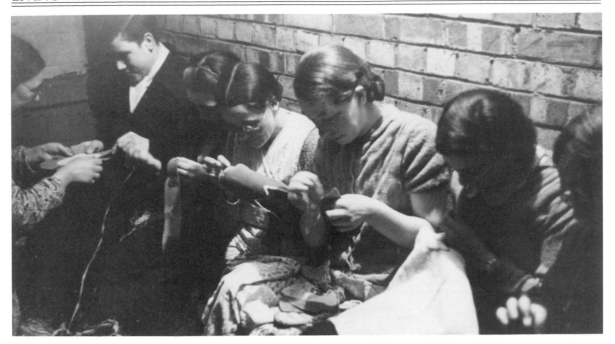

Knitting the night away in a Bermondsey shelter, 29 March 1941. Progressive boroughs like Bermondsey set up evening classes in subjects ranging from drama and needlework to politics, to make sheltering less arduous and sometimes even enjoyable

and an old piano where people were sitting having a singsong, and there was a cinema the other side of the cave. In the tea room there were a couple of tables, where the W.V.S. used to work, and they were selling pies and sandwiches and cakes, and you could get a cup of tea for a penny. Then further along there was the hospital where the children learnt to line up to get their cough mixture, that sort of thing. And then there was a little chapel, and on a Sunday I used to go by the chapel, and the kids would be singing away at their hymns. And there was a bit of luxury, they even put in wash rooms and facilities, like men's and ladies' toilets. So it was quite nice, I enjoyed it.

When the better weather brought the return of the Luftwaffe, Home Intelligence reports noted that Londoners were 'very appreciative' of the new welfare services and that people did not take so long to recover as in the early days of the blitz. The radical changes needed to deal with the direct consequences of the blitz were now complete.

Moreover, a whole new set of ideals was emerging which went much further than the 'welfare' approach that had so far come out of the blitz. People began to see the changes which had been forced on them by the war not just in terms of crises to be overcome but also in terms of new opportunities. In the shelters, for example, there were people regularly gathered together with nothing to do. They could be encouraged to use the time to learn new skills or take up new interests. In Bermondsey – building on its progressive policies of the pre-war years – the borough council set up a range of evening classes in the shelters. In some shelters you could go in any night of the week and find, say, a dressmaking group in one corner, and a drama group in another preparing a play which subsequently the rest of the shelterers would watch. Elsewhere, children would be painting. Once a week there would be a well-attended discussion group dealing with topics ranging from the latest military questions to rights for women. 'Sheltering' was no longer necessarily listless boredom but activity, discussion, even enjoyment. These activities also helped pull people together and strengthen the developing sense of community.

This idea of providing new and positive services – ones which did not just meet people's basic needs but also improved the quality of their lives – was taken up in other ways. In some boroughs, St Pancras for example, travelling libraries were set up to take books out to the people in rest centres, shelters, billets, or even to A.R.P. units. 'We are going to deliver food for the mind to the doors of the people', said the Mayor of St Pancras, reflecting, if rather pompously, this new mood.

Even in the small towns and villages that housed London's evacuees, these new forms of welfare and education sprang up. In London there had been at least some welfare services before the war, especially in progressive boroughs like Bermondsey. But in these sleepy rural retreats, council services were generally regarded with the utmost suspicion, as featherbedding for lame ducks. Now, even here, radical forms of welfare were becoming seen as essential for the war effort. Crèches for the evacuated children and facilities for their mothers were provided to ease the pressure on the 'reception' households. The billeted mother could now go down to a newly-acquired community centre to do her washing and ironing, for the family's meals, or just for a social chat. And the tensions between Londoners and the locals began to disappear. Sometimes dances were held to solidify these new friendships. The sounds of 'The Lambeth Walk' could be heard in places far distant in culture and background from the inner London borough which inspired the thirties hit song. During the spring, poorer children even started to become healthier as they enjoyed the sunshine and fresh country air which rarely penetrated London's slumland. Gladys Strelitz and her children were settling down in Caversham on the outskirts of Reading, and helped by council-run services, were beginning to recover from the shock of the blitz. Gladys recalls:

> At last we felt safe and happy again when we got to Caversham. The council helped us evacuees a lot – they provided us with this place called The Pantry, where we could have a good cheap meal with the children, and all the evacuees from London could have a chat, all together. The meals were really delicious to us in those days. We used to have swede, cheese and onion pie, black pudding, lots of cups of tea. It was all so delicious to us because we'd had to go without for so long. The government paid our billeting allowance and that helped considerably. It helped for little extra things that we didn't have before. And it was good to see the children with a little colour in their cheeks and not looking miserable and tired after the heavy bombing that we had in London.

But, perhaps more important, the changes provided a prototype for the kind of society people felt that they were fighting for. During the blitz there had emerged a new set of ideals which held out a vision of a better world where people's needs were met, where horizons were broadened, and where the pre-war problems of bad housing, poverty and unemployment were eliminated. From now on the government propaganda made much play of the brave new world that would come out of the war. The propaganda film 'Post 23', for example, showed this new spirit of idealism emerging among a group of wardens in Finchley. In reply to a comment from a 'working-class' warden about all the slums and tenements that had come down during the blitz, a 'middle-class' warden states: 'We've got to see the job's done decently this time. If we can work together now, why can't we work together in cleaning up the mess and helping build a better world in which these things can't possibly happen?'

But for the present, the ordeal of mass air attack was not yet over. Throughout the spring of 1941, the night raiders came back regularly, the

Firefighting teams in action in St Paul's Churchyard, May 1941. Modern equipment like turntable ladders enabled the London Fire Brigade to cope with the terrible devastation, which had it occurred earlier might have delivered a knock-out blow to the capital

attacks getting progressively worse. Even with well-organized post-raid services the death and destruction was devastating. Without an effective military defence, the bombers could still wreak tremendous damage.

The severest bombing raid on the capital of the whole blitz came on 10 May. Fires were started from Hammersmith in the west nearly as far as Romford in the east. More civilians were killed than in any other single raid on Britain: 1,436. The House of Commons, Westminster Abbey, the Law Courts, the Royal Mint and the Tower of London were all badly hit. A third of the streets of London were impassable the next morning and 155,000 families found themselves without gas or electricity. Had a raid of such ferocity come nine months earlier, it might have delivered the knock-out blow to the running of the capital and to people's morale of which Hitler dreamed.

The façade of the Salvation Army headquarters at 23 Queen Victoria Street, Blackfriars, collapses in the aftermath of the heaviest attack of the entire blitz on 10 May 1941

But, by now, London had learnt to live with the blitz. The effects of the 10 May raid were cleared up at a speed which would have seemed impossible when the bombings began. The changes that had been implemented – from the greater efficiency to the abandonment of Poor Law methods to the welfare initiatives – made many people's lives tolerable in the face of exceptional difficulties. Emily Fary and her family now felt they could cope with the bombing, however awful it was.

I remember the May 10 raid, the whole of London seemed to be on fire. We'd been down the tube all night, but when we came out in the morning, we had to run through fires which was raging both sides of the streets. And there was hot falling embers pouring down on us. But we weren't as terrified as we used to be because by then, you see, we had got bunks down the tube, and we had a place that was sort of secure for us. We knew that when we got down there we'd have everything we needed to get by, whatever happened on top, whether there was raging fires or bombs falling.

These trials were, however, now over. This terrible raid marked the end of the blitz. Days and then weeks passed, but the Luftwaffe did not return. For a reason that Londoners were yet to understand, Germany had abandoned its mass air attacks. In the capital, the blitz had left much destruction in its wake. But it had also created a new concern with meeting people's needs that would help Londoners pull through the years of hardship ahead, and had given birth to a vision of a better London, a London really worth fighting for.

4
THE ROAD
TO VICTORY

Londoners woke on the morning of June 22 1941 to hear the most dramatic and important news of the war so far. In the early hours of that morning, Germany had invaded Russia. That day, Hitler's army swept towards Moscow, capturing ten thousand prisoners and destroying more than a thousand Soviet aircraft. From now on, the main thrust of the Nazi's *blitzkrieg* would be directed against the Soviet Union.

The eerie peace of London during the last month was explained: the Luftwaffe had flown off to the East. The capital was no longer in the front line of the war, its citizens no longer the target of the relentless German attack. Though Londoners felt an immediate and deep sense of relief, these feelings were tempered by the belief that the Luftwaffe would soon be back. The incredibly rapid advance of the German army through Russia had led many to believe that the Red Army might collapse within weeks. Britain would then be standing alone again.

But during that summer the mood began to change. For, though the Germans were still making substantial advances through Russian territory, they were meeting fierce and courageous resistance. A wave of admiration for the Soviet people and for the Red Army swept the nation. Britain's new ally was turning out to be a powerful and aggressive fighting force. For the first time since Dunkirk, people felt a tinge of optimism. Their thoughts began to turn to victory. Throughout the capital, walls were painted or chalked with the 'V for Victory' sign as Londoners spontaneously took up the B.B.C.'s slogan for the resistance movement in Europe. London's prospects had been transformed.

But Britain was not yet on the road to victory. To get there, her fighting forces had to be far better equipped for modern warfare. As yet, war production remained disappointingly low. Without more tanks and trucks, ships and planes, guns and munitions, radios and radar and a host of other weapons of war, there was no chance of a counter-attack. In addition, the Soviet Union desperately needed shipments of arms and equipment to mount an effective fight against the Nazis on the Eastern Front.

Britain faced a crisis in war production. The whole economy urgently needed to be geared up for war. London's role in overcoming this crisis and putting Britain on the road to victory was to be as critical as it had been in staving off defeat. And the changes that this would bring to every waking hour of every Londoner's life were to be as radical as the changes brought by the blitz itself.

The crisis arose chiefly from the organization and location of industry. The first, and most major, problem stemmed from the fact that London had been Germany's prime target for air attack. While the Germans' bombs had not, in themselves, inflicted significant losses in output, the policies which had been introduced to counter the expected effects of the

Previous pages: Women at war. Assembling sten gun components at the Royal Ordnance Factory, Enfield, Middlesex, in 1943

blitz were holding back war production quite considerably.

In the early stages of the war, the government had desperately tried to avoid placing major orders in 'vulnerable' areas like the London region, preferring, wherever possible, the 'safe' areas of north-west England and Scotland. They feared that if key war industries were concentrated in the capital, the whole programme could be brought to a halt by the Luftwaffe. The result was that, although some orders inevitably ended up in London, the capital's resources were not fully utilized for the war effort. The massive Ford Works at Dagenham in Essex, for example, was starved of virtually any kind of order for military production.

Even after Dunkirk, when the desperate need for a better equipped fighting force first became blindingly obvious, this policy of avoiding London continued. However, by the late summer of 1940, when the minority of workers in the capital who were involved in war production were exhausted from the endless hours at their machines, it was becoming clear that the policy was absurd. The government and the military began to rethink their placements of major orders, now recognizing the fact that there were factories in London still making non-essential products which could easily be switched to war production.

By that stage the classification of 'safe' and 'vulnerable' areas was anyway beginning to seem militarily dubious. The Luftwaffe were now poised along the Continental coastal areas and anywhere in Britain was within their range. Indeed, the military chiefs became concerned that the building of new factories in supposedly 'safe' rural areas would attract the enemy's attention and make them prime targets. Existing factories in urban areas, it was now argued, might be less visible and vulnerable.

All these new considerations led the government to lift the restriction on the development of war industry in London in the early autumn of 1940. But by then the blitz had begun. During the next nine months, London was struggling simply to survive. There was little chance for a shift in the capital's industries to war production. The result was that come the production crisis of the summer of 1941, London was poised for a great expansion in its war effort.

The large-scale engineering and chemical factories were the easiest to draw into the war machine. They had the plant and equipment that enabled mass production for the military once it had been converted from civilian to war products. The Ford foundry at Dagenham was soon working flat out making a wide range of army trucks and gun carriers. In the East End, despite the effects of the blitz, factories managed to turn to war production. Ironically, they often made the most explosive of products, as this area had for almost a century housed the bulk of the capital's noxious chemical industries. Paint factories, though they had been heavily damaged during the bombings because of the inflammable nature of their products, made the switch. Bryant & May, the match makers in Bow, made demolition charges and safety fuses. Albright & Wilson, the chemical firm in Canning Town, became a major shell-filling firm.

But the greatest expansion came in the west and north-western parts of London, where industry in pre-war years had been booming and where, as a result, many of the factories were modern and well equipped. A wide range of war production sprang up; A.E.C. in Southall, for example, turned from making buses to armoured cars carrying six-pounder guns. Easy access to the Midlands, where the air-frame industries were concentrated, led to the expansion of engineering production for the aircraft industry; Napiers in Acton, for example, had gambled on the development of a new engine which was to be used in the mass production of the Typhoon and Tempest fighters.

Much of London's production remained, however, very small-scale in nature. In the north-east of the capital over two-thirds of the engineering firms employed less than fifty people. Gearing this potential output to the war effort was critically important, but coordinating these small and often fiercely independent firms proved much more difficult than drawing in the large engineering firms. The firms were being asked to cooperate with rivals in new joint production plans. Nevertheless, throughout the capital these kinds of adjustments did take place. For example, when the state-run Royal Small Arms Factory in Enfield developed the sten gun – a cheap and easily-produced sub-machine gun – it looked to hundreds of small local workshops for the production. Firms which once had made a glittering array of goods from sewing machines to windscreen wipers were welded together into one long war production line. Lorries travelled between the numerous premises creating a sort of metropolitan conveyer belt.

Perhaps the most remarkable transformation was in the furniture industry of north-east London. Carpenters turned from making chairs, tables, wardrobes and the like to mass producing a wooden plane. The 'Mosquito', as it was called, was the most unusual plane of the war. It was made from sheets of paper-thin plywood and balsa wood, glued together and then heated to form a product as tough as metal but much lighter. These strengthened wooden sheets were then sawn and shaved into the parts of the plane, from the bulk head to the tail piece, from the fuel tanks to the wings. Alf Pearson worked in Wrighton's Mosquito factory in Walthamstow:

July 1944 sees the celebration of Mosquito fuselage No. 1000 built by Wrightons of Walthamstow, one of almost a hundred London based sub-contractors for the 'wooden bomber' the De Havilland Mosquito

It was out of this world really, because kiddies used to make little models, little toys out of this balsa wood and we couldn't believe that we

were using inch-thick balsa wood to make a plane that was going to fly over Germany and be armed. We were most of us skilled cabinet-makers and we used the same sort of tools that we did on furniture – planes, chisels, saws – to make the Mossies. We felt absolutely bucked about it, that we were doing something useful to help us win the war. But to begin with we never thought it would fly.

The end product was, in fact, exceptionally versatile. Used for reconnaissance work, the Mosquito could fly low into enemy territory and fast enough to evade interception. As a night-time bomber, it could carry the same weight of high explosive as a conventional bomber and fly in greater safety at 21,000 feet. And as a small passenger plane, the Mosquito was the fastest in the world – and if you wanted it to go even faster, all you had to do was give it a good wax with furniture polish.

At the same time as existing factories were being turned over to war production, new factories were hastily being built. Often these were on the outskirts of London where sites were easily available. The small towns of Slough, Watford, Hemel Hempstead and Welwyn Garden City expanded rapidly, often recruiting skilled workers from inner London.

Empty premises throughout London were also swiftly converted into factories. Unused basements, cellars, warehouses, even an unfinished London Transport Underground tunnel, were all given a new life. Perhaps the most unexpected of these transformations took place under the Houses of Parliament. While the elected members moved to the House of Lords to carry on with business as usual, underneath the ruined debating chamber of the House of Commons a very different type of business had sprung up. What is called the Guy Fawkes cellar was converted to house a submarine factory whose workers toiled day and night. The whole operation was secret, known about only by Members of Parliament

Two examples of how London was gearing up for the war effort. The Mosquito fuselage shop at Wrightons of Walthamstow (left), which turned from making furniture to making planes and (below) doormen and dukes rub shoulders in the secret submarine factory underneath the House of Commons, 1943

and the staff of the Palace of Westminster who manned the factory in their spare time. Vera Michel-Downes was the factory's welfare officer:

> We had a fantastic atmosphere in the factory, which was really totally classless. We had staff from all walks of life: the policeman, the postman, the fireman, the legal advisors, the secretarial staff, the staff from the House of Lords and the House of Commons, and, of course, close relatives of Members of Parliament. And they all were issued with the same white overalls. The ladies had foldover overalls that tied at the back and the gentlemen had overalls that buttoned down. And they were all working next to each other, and with class disappearing, most of them were on first-name terms and some very good friendships were made.

At last London's industrial potential was being realized for the war production drive. In the meantime, however, the demands from the military for more men and equipment were ever increasing. The Army, engaged in a demanding see-saw campaign in North Africa, and the Royal Navy, fighting a continuous battle against the German U-boat campaign, needed urgently to replace their losses, while the Royal Air Force, now under less pressure to defend Britain against the Luftwaffe, wanted to escalate their raids on German territory. This all placed a tremendous burden on industry. Output had to be increased while at the same time experienced workers had to be released to join the armed forces.

To achieve this required radical changes in methods of industrial production and far more state control over people's working lives. By this stage of the war, the Labour ministers in the coalition government – who were politically committed to such a strategy – were in influential positions on the home front. In particular, Ernest Bevin, the bull-headed pre-war leader of the Transport & General Workers Union, was in charge at the Ministry of Labour. Bevin set about gearing up the war economy by passing the Essential Work Orders Act. This gave the government unprecedented powers to direct workers into 'essential' work and, in turn, required firms classified as 'essential' to meet certain minimum wages and safety standards. This was the first of many changes that would combine greater control over people's working lives with improvements in their working conditions. But this measure, in itself, was insufficient. The government estimated that an extra two million recruits were needed nationally either for the armed forces or for the additional output required from the war industries.

The government, faced with this acute shortage of labour, turned to all possible sources. The Londoners who had been rounded up and interned as 'aliens' after Dunkirk now found that they were back at work making guns, tanks and essential products, and in their spare time were on duty in the Home Guard. Jewish refugee, Klaus Hinrichsen, had been interned on the Isle of Man:

> In the summer of 1941, I was released and came back to my little attic flat in Hampstead. The feeling in London had changed, refugees were

now accepted, and the war effort needed everyone's help, particularly people with any skills. I was directed by the Labour Exchange to a firm in Sunbury-on-Thames, making chemical products. I contacted a number of continental chemists I knew who knew all about ersatz, substitute materials, and we took over part of a small factory, and produced substitute shoe polishes, substitute detergents and substitute materials which at that time were something completely new. I felt this was in some way a contribution to the war effort, because we had to make things without the old raw materials – the ships bringing them to Britain weren't getting through. Then one day I went to the Home Guard barracks in St John's Wood, and asked whether I could sign on. They enlisted me, and very soon I found myself a sharp shooter and in possession of a rifle, guarding vital installations like the B.B.C. and viaducts around London.

Recruiting offices were set up all over the British Empire to encourage volunteers to do their bit for Britain. More than 15,000 arrived from the West Indies alone, some of them gravitating to the London area to work in munitions factories and with ground crews in the R.A.F. There was even a handful of black air raid wardens in the St Pancras area and black auxiliary firemen.

But for the vast majority of this extra labour there was only one source – women. From the start of the war, droves of young women had gone vol-

Black air raid wardens in St Pancras, 1942. Recruiting offices attracted volunteers from all over the British Empire to do their bit for Britain

untarily into the factories. The government now made it compulsory. At the beginning of December 1941, conscription for women was introduced for the first time in British history. This required all unmarried women aged between nineteen and thirty to register for war work of some kind. Some were conscripted into the forces, though the shortfall here was small because of the large number of volunteers for the women's services. Most of the conscripted women were directed to work in essential industries.

From now on, women moved from a marginal to a central position in the war production drive. Whether in Enfield putting together the intricate mechanism of the sten gun, or in Dagenham lifting the molten metal casts from the foundry, or in Chiswick assembling a Halifax bomber at London Transport's converted workshops, women were doing jobs previously thought beyond their capabilities. For many it was a liberating experience. Odette Lesley was directed to work in the Pullman Springs factory in Hendon which had transferred from making fittings for luxury railway carriages to the production of fuel tanks for Spitfires:

Many women found themselves conscripted into essential industries to solve the manpower crisis and boost the war production drive. Below: *A woman operates a screw-thread machine at the converted London Passenger Transport Board Works, in Acton, 1941.* Far right: *Women lower an engine into place, a job that only men would have been allowed to do before the war*

I was terrified to begin with because I had never even picked up a spanner before and I thought I'll never learn it, what am I going to do. And you found that the men were resentful and wary of the women because they'd never worked with women before. But I had to learn it, it was war work and gradually I learnt the things properly and I almost started to enjoy it, not just because of the work but because I knew it was war work and therefore it was of use to the country. Of course, the longer we were there we got more and more proficient in the job and we became quite confident. Because the men and women were doing exactly the same job we felt just as good as the boys. And as new men

came into the plant very often we were teaching them the job. They would be like I was originally, a bit terrified and also a bit embarrassed because a woman knew the job and they didn't.

In some workplaces women were so much in control that they started to adopt some of the old male traditions, like initiation ceremonies and practical jokes, and sprang them on young male recruits – as Charlie Draper discovered when he first began work at a sten gun factory in Peckham:

The majority of workers in the factory were women, all the men were away in the forces. And the women more or less took over everything. I used to get teased a lot by the women in there, sending you out to the shops for pregnant tarts, and sending you down to the stores for a long wait or some elbow grease. The women were even doing the initiation ceremonies, like the men used to. Myself, I got my trousers taken down, and my private parts sprayed with lacquer, and I spent a couple of hours sitting in the toilets, with a tin of thinners, washing it off.

In the armed forces, women moved out of administrative 'welfare' jobs. Though they were never allowed or encouraged to fight on the military front, increasingly there were new opportunities to join 'active' units on the home front. Nina Hibbin, who had now ended her association with Home Intelligence out of disgust with the government's manipulation of the information she provided, was called up in the W.A.A.F. and became a flight mechanic at Hendon. Like many other women in the forces, she found her work opened up a whole new world of learning and skill that had previously been the exclusive domain of men:

I joined the W.A.A.F. because I really wanted to do something with my hands to learn a trade, a mechanical trade. I chose engines and I was actually on Spitfires, and used to service the whole thing. But when I was on this mechanic's course to learn how to do it, it was like a most amazing revelation. I'd no idea how an engine worked before, I couldn't imagine how I'd got to the age of twenty, jumping on and off buses without understanding this marvellous theory about how things worked. To some extent it changed my whole approach, which up to then had been to have a good time and cheek the officers. And suddenly here was this whole new field of work and thought. Once I actually got into trouble for not being at a make-up lecture and being instead in the library swotting up mechanics. And really, that was the part of the W.A.A.F. that I enjoyed the most.

Many London girls were now hoisting the enormous balloons forming the barrage above the capital to discourage low level and dive bomb attacks, work for which they had previously been thought too weak. Many found themselves on ack ack units, servicing and loading the guns, though they were still not allowed to pull the triggers. And although during the winter of 1941 those who were on the ack ack guns spent most of their time in exercises as the German planes were still busy on the Eastern Front, in the years to come these female teams played an important role in keeping the Luftwaffe at bay.

These changes began to challenge the traditional conceptions of what was 'women's work'. The requirements of war were, however, to bring yet further changes in attitudes to the appropriate role for women. For just a few days after conscription for young unmarried women had been introduced, the whole scale of the war escalated rapidly.

On Sunday, 7 December, the Japanese air force bombed the United States fleet at anchor in Pearl Harbor, Hawaii. This action brought America into the war and Britain declared war on Japan. In the long term, America's involvement would prove to be of immense value to the Allied war effort. The most immediate impact, however, came from Japan's entry into the war. Japanese troops swiftly marched into Malaya, opening up a whole new battle zone in the Far East. This put even more pressure on Britain's overstretched war machine. Now, in addition to sending air-craft, tanks and weapons to Russia and to the Middle East, men and mat-erials had to be diverted to south-east Asia. In order both to release more men to fight and to provide munitions for the widening conflict, more and more women had to be drawn into the workforce.

In the pre-war years, it had generally been accepted that young unmar-ried women should work for a wage – but this did not hold for older married women with domestic responsibilities. The war changed all that. People no longer thought that women were 'doing their bit' for the war effort by looking after their homes. Though many women had volun-teered for war work, the numbers were not enough. Older women, with-out the responsibility of children, now had by law to register for work, ini-tially up to forty, then up to forty-five and eventually to fifty.

The most radical shift in attitudes, however, related to the role of

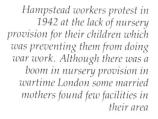

Hampstead workers protest in 1942 at the lack of nursery provision for their children which was preventing them from doing war work. Although there was a boom in nursery provision in wartime London some married mothers found few facilities in their area

women with children. In the pre-war years, a woman's duty was seen to be first and foremost to care for her children. Despite this, during the first years of the war many mothers with older children joined the expanding workforce. There was now increasing pressure – often from women themselves – to recruit mothers with young children. At the beginning of 1942 a 'women's parliament' at Conway Hall in London demanded more nurseries. This was followed up later in the year by nursery demonstrations: in Hampstead mothers and their children marched with placards proclaiming 'Nurseries for kids, war work for mothers'. 'Hampstead mothers stage baby riot to demand more day nurseries' ran the headline in *Picture Post*, the popular radical illustrated weekly. The *Daily Mirror* reported that in Cricklewood there were scores of mothers willing to go into the local Halifax bomber factory if only nurseries were provided.

The official response was very divided. In some London boroughs, Ealing for example, the medical officers strongly opposed the growth of nurseries, believing such care to be bad for the children. The Ministry of Labour, meanwhile, was running a campaign to recruit mothers into the factories. Eventually, the needs of industry prevailed and nursery provision started to expand rapidly. And the great experiment worked. Mothers could contribute to the war effort knowing that their children were safe, while the children often benefitted from the educational and welfare provisions at the nursery centres. The Ministry of Information, appreciating the need for more workers, was not slow to sing the praises of the new nurseries in films like 'Five and Under'. Eventually, eighty per cent of London's married women were employed, although nursery provision, despite the growth, remained inadequate.

Women whose children were too young to be placed in a nursery often did part-time war work at home. One of them was Emily Golder, now married and with a small baby in Finchley.

I noticed this part-time job advertised to assemble aircraft parts at home so I decided to do that. The money was a great help, and I also felt I was doing my bit towards the war. I used to load the pram up with the chrome parts from the garage where I collected them and wheel the pram home, my son would be sitting on top, and all the bits and pieces on the bottom. That kept me busy for a couple of hours each day on top of looking after the baby, but you just took it in your stride.

At the same time as women were being sucked into the workforce to solve the manpower crisis, attention was also being focussed on the industries making consumer products for the home market, both essential items like food and less essential items like furniture. Many workers from these industries had already moved or had been directed by the state into war production and as a consequence output was well below the pre-war levels. Before more workers could be switched, the problem of shortages had to be tackled more effectively – a problem that during the early part of 1942 had been made increasingly urgent by the escalation of the war. Japanese victories in the Far East had cut off traditional supplies of rubber, tin, tea and sugar, and a spate of German U-boat attacks following

America's entry into the war had led to a sharp increase in shipping losses.

Rationing, which had been introduced early in the war for a number of items of food, notably butter, bacon and sugar, was extended and intensified. During 1942, many foods – including sweets and chocolate – were rationed. The precise rations varied each month according to shipping losses and seasonal supplies. On average, the adult weekly ration was 2oz of tea, 4oz of butter or margarine, 2oz of cooking fat, 8oz of jam, honey or marmalade, 8oz of sugar, 2oz of cheese, 4oz of bacon or ham, 2½ pints of milk (when it was rationed), and 1½d. worth of meat, which would buy about two small chops or half a pound of stewing steak. In addition, each month a person was entitled to 20 'points' worth of tinned goods – which would buy, for example, a tin of spam, or five tins of baked beans – and one packet of dried eggs. Bread, vegetables, fruit, offal and fish were unrationed but, apart from bread, potatoes and a few basic vegetables, like carrots and cabbage, these goods were a rarity. The consequent diet seemed to all but the poorest London families to be dull and meagre.

The clothes ration, introduced a year earlier, was also tightened up. The basic clothes ration from the spring of 1942 only allowed a man to buy, for example, an overcoat once every seven years, a pullover every five years, a pair of trousers and a jacket every two years, a pair of pants every two years, a shirt every twenty months and a pair of shoes every eight months. The restrictions on women were equally spartan.

But there was a limit to which the problems of shortages could be solved by squeezing the consumer. The government were forced into turning to control the production of goods as well as their consumption. In March 1942, the government introduced 'Utility' goods. This scheme specified simple and practical designs for a whole range of goods, from suits to settees, so that the same quantity of goods could be produced by fewer workers. So, for example, the remaining furniture-makers in north London now had to make articles to a simple pattern, without time-wasting frills. As a result, it was possible to go some way at least to alleviating the furniture crisis which had been created by the blitz and at the same time to allow more carpenters to go off and make aircraft.

These principles applied to the manufacture of a whole range of goods: crockery, pots, and pans, boots and shoes, carpets, domestic electrical appliances – the list is almost endless. Perhaps most important for the consumer was the effect on clothing. The number of basic designs was limited to encourage long production runs, and each design would exclude trimmings such as embroidery or the wasteful use of materials through, for example, pleats or turn-ups. For many Londoners, these changes brought the benefit of reliable quality goods at a reasonable price. But some, the rich in particular, resented their diminishing range of choice and the lack of exclusive and expensive designs, the wearing of which had propped up their social superiority.

The government tried other ways of alleviating shortages. In particular, a strong anti-consumer, anti-spending ethos was developed. This was done partly through the work of National Savings. Most streets in Lon-

Far Left: *Families hard at work converting a Chelsea bomb site into allotments in June 1942. Vegetable patches, chicken runs and pigsties appeared in every spare bit of land in London, as part of the 'Dig for Victory' campaign, promoted by posters such as these (above) which plastered London in the middle years of the war. The keynote was self-sufficiency*

Left: *A model displays the look of 1943 – a striped rayon dress for which seven coupons were required. Plain utility clothes like these were one way of cutting the costs of consumer goods and channelling resources towards war production*

don, and virtually every school, would have a savings club and each London borough joined in these savings campaigns with War Weapons weeks. But the main aim was not, in fact, to raise money but to stop people wanting to spend it: an aim clearly demonstrated by the 'squanderbug', a propaganda cartoon portrayal of the sort of 'thoughtless' people that lavish their money on themselves rather than handing it over to the government to spend on weapons.

This was a task made somewhat more difficult by the American G.I.s now beginning to arrive in the capital with their aura of Hollywood glamour. As an ordinary G.I. earned four times the wages of his British counterpart, and as he also had easy access through American bases to tinned foods, cigarettes and 'candies', which were strictly rationed elsewhere, he presented an enviable sight to many Londoners. But the standard of living of the G.I. was simply unavailable to local residents.

Instead, the British were encouraged to be more self-sufficient. Government departments ran a number of highly effective propaganda campaigns aimed at helping people to get by on their spartan rations. The 'make-do-and-mend' campaign, for example, gave practical advice on extending the life of old clothes. Sewing classes sprang up across London showing women how, for example, to reverse a collar or to make a child's skirt out of an old pair of trousers. In the home, improvization became the watchword. Those setting up home, in particular, had sometimes to make do with old crates for tables or an empty dried milk tin as a measuring jug.

Increasingly, every hour was occupied in one way or another in supporting the war effort. If you weren't at work itself, or mending worn-out clothes, or transforming an old piece of metal into a curtain rail, then you should be sorting out the rubbish for salvage for re-use in the war industries. Old bones, so the government propaganda claimed, could become the glue for a Spitfire, old newspapers could make shell cups, waste fats could be used for explosives. All sorts of gimmicks were used to sustain interest in the salvage campaign. Bermondsey and Bethnal Green challenged eacy other to paper-collecting competitions. Paddington ran a 'Mile of Keys' campaign to collect a million keys. Often the keenest collectors were children, and the Brownies managed to pay for an aircraft with their salvaged jam jars. Later the government started a 'Cog' scheme making children official salvage collectors – or 'cogs'. They could sometimes be heard singing their official Cog song, 'There'll always be a dustbin' sung to the tune of 'There'll always be an England'.

After sorting out the salvage, Londoners were expected to 'dig for victory'. Allotments sprouted up all over the capital from bombed sites to the local council park, from the Albert Memorial gardens in Kensington to the moat of the Tower of London. The vegetables produced were treasured, supplementing as they did the meagre rations. Keeping pigs and chickens, and sometimes rabbits and goats, became all the craze. Surface shelters, no longer in use for protection against the bombs, became hen houses. The snorting and snuffling of pigs could be heard in unlikely places like Pall Mall, where the swimming bath of the Ladies Carlton Club was converted into a giant pig sty. Often these activities drew people together. Neighbours would realize, for example, that if they got together and combined all their vegetable waste, they would have enough to feed a pig. Charlie Draper and his family were now back in Peckham, where they turned the back garden into a mini farmyard.

> We used to keep a few chickens and a couple of geese, a couple of ducks and nine rabbits in the garden. We'd feed them on scraps from the kitchen, potato peelings, cabbage leaves, any old thing. They used to help supplement the rations. On special occasions we'd have chicken or rabbit for dinner, fresh from the back garden, go out there and see what took your fancy, and it tasted a bit better than the two ounces of corned beef that we got on the rations. Dad might sell a couple over the pub and get his beer money, or one or two of the neighbours used to have them.

From all these changes a new spirit was emerging which valued cooperation above competition. There was, in addition, a far greater emphasis on equality. In particular, many of the rich were losing some of their privileges. For example, miles of wrought-iron railings, which had previously guarded their privacy, were removed from around their West End squares, parks and gardens for use in munitions. This sort of social levelling was greeted with enthusiasm by many Londoners who were prepared to put up with hardship as long as they felt that everyone was making sacrifices. Home Intelligence reports on Londoners noted, for example, resentment against those who were able to get round the rationing regulations by dining out at expensive West End restaurants, and against those who wasted petrol on pleasure trips to the country. Indeed by the spring of 1942, discontent that the hardships brought by the war were not fairly shared was so widespread that the government restricted petrol supplies for pleasure motoring and placed a five-shilling limit on restaurant meals. Remaining displays of extravagance faded, though in practice they were never completely wiped out.

But, most important, these new values demanded that everyone must do their utmost for the community and the nation rather than for themselves. It was 'total war' and that required 'total' effort from everybody. Whether at home, in the factory or in the office, this meant incessant work for the war effort.

All these pressures, however, took their toll. Women, in particular, found that after a long shift bent over a factory machine, they would then spend hours queuing for their food rations, and then yet more time trying to transform a handful of ingredients into a family meal. Although Ministry of Food campaigns featuring characters like Potato Pete and Dr Carrot offered good advice on different ways of making a nutritious meal out of, for example, a few potatoes and a cabbage, in practice many mothers found it difficult and time-consuming to produce meals that their children were prepared to eat.

Many women were becoming increasingly tired or exhausted. This, in turn, caused problems for the war economy. A tired worker is a slow and inefficient worker and an exhausted worker is more likely to be late or even absent. Indeed, during 1942 levels of absenteeism did begin to grow. Odette Lesley recalls the strain of the long hours spent at work: 'We worked terribly long hours. We had to work a sixty-hour week which was compulsory. You were dreadfully tired and your work was bound to suffer. You used to crawl out of the factory. I mean three days a week we used to do eight in the morning till eight at night, and your breaks were very short.'

There could, however, be no easing up. On the military front, Britain was suffering continuing defeats, especially in south-east Asia where Singapore had fallen in February 1942. The armed forces needed more weapons to make up for their heavy losses. The whole war effort was threatened unless output increased. But unless the workforce's morale and fitness could be kept up, output, far from increasing, was at risk of slumping. Concern for the welfare of industrial workers began to mount.

Managements, under pressure from the Ministry of Labour, started to improve working conditions. The buzzing and grinding of machinery on the factory floor was increasingly drowned by the sounds of popular music. 'Progressive' managements relayed new B.B.C. radio programmes like 'Worker's Playtime' and 'Music While You Work' over loudspeakers several times a day. The women would often time their actions on the machines to coincide with the rhythm of the music, thereby making the routine more enjoyable and at the same time helping to keep up their rate of work. Mary Hankins worked in a munitions factory in Acton: 'We were on the assembly line which wasn't much fun itself but the music helped us to work faster and keep happy. Everyone would be singing along when "Music While You Work" was on. Sometimes I'd start everybody going, get on my chair, and lead them into "The Lambeth Walk" and "My Old Man". The spirit in the factories was fantastic.'

At the same time, more substantial changes were made to conditions on the shop floor. These were much needed for the black-out, which was imposed on all premises, be they factories or private homes, often created

Mary Hankins on piano with The Actonians – her works band at C.A.V. Electrical. They gave regular canteen concerts in the Acton area. Music in the factories was part of a new management strategy to boost war production

severe problems with ventilation and lighting. Health and safety conditions began to improve, though progress was rather slow. Firms, under tremendous pressure to fulfill rushed orders, found it difficult to find a time when production could be discontinued so that improvements could be made. But the Ministry of Labour forced factories with more than 250 employees to appoint welfare workers. As a result, an increasing number of large London factories set up sick rooms or started to employ doctors and nurses.

But, perhaps most important, many factories opened canteens for their workers. These often turned out to be far more than halls just for eating but leisure and social centres as well. During the meal, the workers would sometimes put on their own entertainments, and afterwards the tables and chairs would be cleared away so that they could sing and dance through the rest of their lunch break. Mary Hankins remembers:

> We formed a song and dance act in the factory. I was on the piano. We started off in the canteen, then we began performing in all the factory canteens around Acton. They'd tap their knives and forks to the music, and it would be nothing for them to clear away a few tables and have a knees up. Then the B.B.C. heard that we were pretty good and we did a Worker's Playtime concert at our factory. Everyone thought that was wonderful.

For similar reasons, entertainment outside the workplace became extremely important. On their nights off from work, young women would regularly go to the dance halls: the Hammersmith Palais, the Streatham Locarno, the Paramount in Tottenham Court Road or the Lyceum in Ilford. These were their escape routes to relaxation. Everywhere the dance floors were packed with girls from the factories and offices, and servicemen of every nationality. For the young men and women dancing the nights away, these hours of light-hearted fun became

London girls dance with black G.I.s in 1944. Dancing was one of the great escapes that helped lift the spirits of a capital which spent most waking hours working for the war effort

treasured times away from the pressures of work and from the stark reality of a world at war.

The desire for a cheerful and communal escapism was reflected in a great demand for noisy and silly dances in which everyone could join, like Boomps-a-Daisy, the Conga and the Palais Glide. Odette Lesley often went to the Hammersmith Palais:

> Of course they used to play all the dances we liked: the waltzes, the quicksteps and the fox trots. But what we really used to wait for was the Palais Glide, this was the one we knew was going to get everyone together. You'd get strung out across the ballroom, great lines of boys and girls, and then they'd start to play, 'Horsey, horsey, don't you stop, just let your feet go clippety clop. Your tail goes swish and the wheels go round, giddyup, we're homeward bound.' And, of course, that sort of dance was marvellous, because it got the boys and girls mixed up together, and there was no shyness any more. Then we'd go in groups, and we'd sit around a table and have coffee and we'd talk. It was a great thing for us, it gave us an impetus to go to work the next morning.

The authorities increasingly recognized the importance of leisure as a 'reward' for the hard work put into the war effort. In the summer of 1942, local councils throughout the capital organized all sorts of special attractions to encourage people to spend their holidays at home and thereby free transport for military use. The London County Council laid on an extensive programme of events to make 'Stay-at-home holidays Play-at-Home'. Every evening there would be a choice of thirteen different open-air entertainments with everything from stand-up comedians to Shakespeare. Every swimming pool had its own gala, every open space from Hackney's Victoria Park to Clapham Common had a fair or fête. On the hot summer evenings there was often dancing in the parks. In outer London, there were similar, if less extensive, programmes of events. The borough of Barnes, for example, held displays of physical training, band concerts, 'comic' cricket matches, a Punch and Judy show, and an Olde Worlde Fayre.

These events provided precious moments of distraction from the worries of war. For in the summer of 1942 Britain's performance on the military front continued to be marked by a string of defeats, especially in North Africa. In June, Tobruk was captured by the German commander Rommel and 33,000 Allied troops were taken as prisoners of war. There was bitter criticism from the battalions in North Africa over the unreliability and inferiority of their equipment. Many blamed British industry and, as a consequence, called for fundamental changes.

Indeed, the very basis of British society – capitalism – was coming under attack. Home Intelligence reports noted, with some alarm, that socialist ideals were taking hold, especially in the capital. One reason for this was the continued support for the Soviet Union. When 'Tanks for Russia' weeks were introduced in 1942 – in which all military equipment made was sent to the Eastern Front – Soviet popularity was becoming so great that there was often a boom in production in London factories. This admiration for the Soviet Union was reinforced by the heroic resistance against the Nazi advance, especially the Red Army's brave stand against the Germans at Stalingrad. The stark contrast between Britain's apparent military weakness and the apparent strength of the 'worker's state' led people to be far more critical of the nation's way of organizing itself. This new, radical mood spread far beyond those who had traditionally been socialists. The Liberal, Sir William Beveridge – whose report on post-war social security was to make him a national figure overnight – argued in an article in *The Times*: 'We have left vital production in the hands of individuals whose duty it was to consider not solely the needs of the nation in war but the interests of shareholders and of what would be the position of their business after the war. . . . The time calls for the State to take direct responsibility for the control of vital industries'.

The new mood was particularly strong amongst factory workers who suddenly found themselves in a very powerful bargaining position. Throughout the first year of the war, high unemployment continued to blight Londoners' working lives, but now there was not just full employment but a shortage of labour. The workforce could start to dictate their terms.

Out of these demands for change grew a radical new form of decision-making: the Joint Production Committee. Some of the first J.P.C.s, as they were known, were set up in the state-run Royal Ordnance factories, which in London were based at Woolwich, Waltham Abbey and Enfield. These committees consisted of equal numbers of workers – elected by their fellow workers – and management. From then on, the J.P.C.s had to be consulted on all aspects of the production process and this brought many changes to the factory floor. Often these changes handed over much more responsibility and control to the ordinary worker, whether over small but sensitive issues, such as when to take tea breaks or over more important matters, such as the design of machine tools. Sometimes the changes resulted in improved piece rates or output bonuses for the workers. Overall, they generally resulted in increases in efficiency and output.

Even in firms without formalized consultation with shopfloor workers, there were often new opportunities for people who were not part of the traditional management structure to make a significant impact on production. Whether in white-collar or blue-collar jobs, workers found a much greater receptiveness to new ideas. Low-grade or formally unqualified workers, who nevertheless had skill and imagination, were much more likely to be promoted to positions of responsibility than in the pre-war years. Len Jones, who left school without academic qualifications, had by 1942 become the manager of a unit of technical designers and draughtsmen at Precision Grinding in Mitcham:

I was an East End boy, and I'd taken a few courses and dreamed I might be a draughtsman, but I never really thought it would happen. Then when I started at Precision Grinding not only was I a draughtsman but they gave me the opportunity to design, which wouldn't have happened had it not been for the war. I worked day in and day out on a mechanism to help us bomb targets with greater accuracy and it was quickly taken up. Then, very rapidly, within a few months, they gave me control of the design office, there were twelve or fourteen draughtsmen and five or six lady tracers.

In many areas of London life, traditional hierarchies based on status and class began to be replaced by appointments on the basis of merit. This is shown nowhere more clearly than in the Home Guard. The 'Colonel Blimps' of the First World War, who had often been in charge in 1940, were replaced by a new breed of young men, up-to-date with the modern methods of war. Private training schools like Osterley, initially frowned upon by the authorities, became incorporated into the official work of the Home Guard. Realistic mock battles were held in the bombed-out areas of the capital: the City, Stepney, West Ham and the Isle of Dogs. At weekends, different detachments of the London Home Guard could be seen fiercely fighting in the streets and practising techniques of urban warfare. In the summer of 1942, it still seemed that the threat of invasion might resurface. But soon the war was to change course.

All the changes in industry – from those that increased the recruitment of women and reduced consumer demand to those which began to challenge the very heart of the old private enterprise system – were producing startling results. Production in London's war industries boomed, part of an upturn in the war economy throughout Britain. By the autumn of 1942 output of military equipment was dramatically higher than the level in the summer of 1941, when the production crisis had been so urgent. For example, the number of tanks rolling off the assembly lines had more

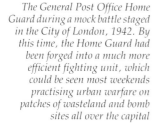

The General Post Office Home Guard during a mock battle staged in the City of London, 1942. By this time, the Home Guard had been forged into a much more efficient fighting unit, which could be seen most weekends practising urban warfare on patches of wasteland and bomb sites all over the capital

than doubled, as had the number of machine guns. The number of small rifles turned out was a staggering twenty-five times higher. New equipment, developed since the summer of 1941, was also flowing from the factories at a remarkable rate; for example, 500,000 sub-machine guns – such as the sten gun – were made in the last three months of 1942. At the same time, imports of military equipment from America were increasing. This all meant that the Allied forces gradually became far better prepared for the fight against the well-equipped Nazi divisions.

In the late autumn of 1942, the benefits began to be reaped. On 2 November, the British Eighth Army, equipped with around four times as many tanks as the German forces, defeated Rommel decisively at El Alamein and thereby turned the tide of the war in North Africa. In London, church bells rang out across the city – in celebration and not, as would have been the case two years earlier, because the Nazis had invaded Britain. At last there was a light at the end of the tunnel.

But for Londoners there could be no complacency. The start of 1943 brought the first raids on London by the Luftwaffe since the blitz. The bombings were in retaliation for an intensive Allied air attack on Berlin. They brought tragedy again to London. One of the bombs scored a direct hit on a primary school in Catford killing thirty-eight children. Londoners felt disturbed by the raids, and a few panicked. On one evening the siren went off while people were queuing for shelter under Bethnal Green tube station and there was a stampede for the stairs; quite unlike people's calm behaviour during the later stages of the blitz itself. In the ensuing crush, 173 people died. This time, however, the scale of the German attack was minor and the British defences – which had been substantially improved with radar on the fighter planes and new anti-aircraft 'rocket projectors' in the ack ack units – were far more successful. After only two raids in January and one in March, the Luftwaffe gave up. Even so, Londoners had been reminded that Allied victories in distant fields and deserts had not meant an end to danger at home.

The Home Intelligence secret reports on morale noted that most people in London desperately hoped that there would be a swift end to the war, and that a 'second front' would now be opened up in France to push Germany back from the west. Indeed, a direct assault on northern Europe was favoured by the United States, but under Churchill's insistence the Allies adopted a strategy which took a much more long-term view of events: first, the North African campaign was to be pursued and won, followed only then by the battle in Europe. The war was set to last a lot longer and the government had to persuade people that it was essential to keep on working flat out.

A spate of propaganda films extolling the factory worker were produced, films which contrasted sharply with the Chaplinesque portrayal of the working class prior to the war. The main theme was how the fighting forces were utterly dependent on all this effort at home. A regular series of films, called 'The Worker and the Warfront', was set up for distribution in factories. Others, like 'Desert Victory' – an account of the victory at El Alamein – were huge box office hits. The tireless work and good spirits of women, and in particular young women, were often the focus of much praise, in films like 'The Night Shift' or 'Millions like Us'. Whereas at the beginning of the war women had been portrayed as a rather vulnerable breed, nervously sipping cups of tea during air raids, now they were celebrated as the boiler-suited heroines of the war – the mechanics, the engineers, the dustmen and the drivers that kept the home front going. Odette Lesley alternated her trips to the dance halls with visits to the cinema:

> We used to go to the cinema whenever we could find time because the cinema, along with dancing, was certainly the biggest leisure pursuit that we loved. And we found that the jobs we were doing, with these awful machines, were being portrayed in the British films like 'This Happy Breed'. And we could identify with the people in them, because this was reality as opposed to the old Hollywood glamour that we used to escape into. We wanted reality now, we wanted to be recognized. We wanted everyone who saw the film to see what we were really doing. And in these films that is how it was, and we were really thrilled. We used to sit there and think, 'Look at that actress, she's working on a machine like I do.' And it really almost gave a bit of glamour to what we were doing, despite the miserable job that it was, and this was very uplifting. Maybe it was a type of propaganda but if it was it was excellent and it worked.

The greatest morale booster, however, was always success on the battlefield and by the late spring of 1943 the military rewards for people's efforts were becoming more visible. On 12 May, the Allies finally overcame the last of the German and Italian troops in North Africa. That summer Germany was in retreat, not only in the Mediterranean but also in the east where the Red Army was pushing the Nazi divisions back towards the Fatherland. With her ally, Italy, in internal turmoil, the time was ripe to strike while the enemy was weak. Serious planning for an Allied invasion of northern Europe now began.

In August, the Allied commanders made their final decision to go ahead with a sea-borne invasion of northern France. But there was much to do before that was possible. A vast array of equipment would be needed to give any chance of success for the proposed landings. But, because of the pressures of other military campaigns, the production of this equipment had hardly got underway.

The key role that the capital was to play in these preparations completed the reversal in attitudes towards London at war that had been taking place during the course of the war. At the beginning, London's industrial capacity had been deliberately under-used. During the middle phase of the war, the pressure of war production had necessitated a rapid expansion in the capital's war industries. Now, as the conflict reached its climax, London was to be at the heart of a great production drive to win the war.

The invasion plan, code-named Operation Overlord, involved landing about a million men on the beaches of Normandy. The Allied commanders saw the key to success in flexibility. Hitler expected an Allied counter-attack and was building up defences and troop reinforcements at strategic points along the coast. The Allies had to be able to land in Normandy at a few days' notice. This military tactic posed tremendous technical problems for the engineering industries.

While the troops themselves could be landed easily enough anywhere, they only formed an effective fighting force if at the same time tanks, jeeps, trucks, field guns, anti-aircraft guns, flame throwers and all the other military hardware of a modern army were swiftly ferried ashore. To do this, the transporting ships had to be protected while they were unloading from the often rough waters of the Atlantic. And then, there had to be a constant flow of supplies to service all this equipment. In particular, there had to be petrol. All these considerations posed far more difficult problems. A top secret plan – code-named Mulberry – was drawn up. The components for two floating Mulberry harbours would be built in Britain, towed by tugs across the Channel and assembled off the Normandy beaches. Each floating Mulberry would be twice the size of the harbour at Dover. At the same time, a petrol pipeline would be laid along the seabed from Britain to France. It was code-named Pluto, for Pipe Line Under The Ocean.

The final gathering-point in Britain for all this equipment was the Channel coast, meaning that the lion's share of the work had to be based in the south of England. As London was by far the biggest industrial centre of the area, the capital had to play a pivotal role in the development and production of the special equipment needed for Operation Overlord.

The difficulties this presented for London's industries were immense, partly because of the sheer scale and speed of the production needs, and partly because of the enormity of the technical problems of developing equipment for sea-borne invasion. For example, ways of waterproofing and adapting a wide range of military transport had to be tested, and mile upon mile of petrol pipe strong enough to withstand the ocean had to be devised.

However, the greatest problems were caused by the Mulberry harbours themselves. Nothing of the nature of a floating harbour had ever been constructed before. The core of the plan was to build enormous, hollow concrete units, or 'caissons', which could be towed across the Channel and then joined together and sunk so as to form breakwaters and harbour walls. A floating pier, joined to the shore by a floating roadway, would then be placed within the 'harbour'.

These huge caissons for the harbour wall were technically the most ambitious part of the plan. The largest would be over 60 feet high and 200 feet long and even the smallest were 25 feet high and 176 feet long. As construction got underway, three large London docks were drained to house over half the estimated work: the East India Docks, the southern section of the Surrey Docks, and part of the Tilbury Docks were in this way transformed into a mosaic of building sites. At the same time, along the banks of the Thames, huge basins were dug out to form temporary dry docks. Eight sites were chosen between Belvedere and Erith on the south side, around Grays on the north bank, and in Barking Creek. The sites for both these projects were fraught with danger, for nobody knew

With preparations for Operation Overlord nearly complete in 1944, the Germans were hurrying to perfect one of their most deadly secret weapons – the V-2 (above) – the first long-range rocket ever. In what became a race against time, hollow concrete units, called Phoenix Caissons (right), were towed across the Channel to form part of a floating harbour for the invasion force. Moored in the foreground are landing craft to be used on D-day

for sure whether the old walls of the drained docks, unexposed since Victorian times, would collapse, or whether the newly-built basins would cave in.

But as this great production drive gained momentum in the autumn of 1943, a new threat was emerging. British Intelligence had pieced together evidence which suggested that Hitler was preparing a pre-emptive attack with a secret long-range weapon. Their reports indicated that the Germans were developing a pilotless aircraft and that ramps, suspected of being launching pads, were being constructed on the Channel coast around Pas de Calais. The lines of fire from these ramps all passed over London.

British Intelligence was firmly on the right track in its deductions. Hitler was, indeed, planning a counter-offensive. From an early stage in the war, Germany had been developing new methods of bombing which exploited the latest scientific and technological developments. There were three parts to this programme.

First, German scientists were testing a pilotless aeroplane with a one-ton high explosive warhead. When over its target, the engine would automatically cut out and the whole plane would plummet and explode on impact. The V-1, as it was eventually called, was in effect a 'flying' bomb. Then there was the V-2, the first long-range rocket ever developed. This would be fired out of the earth's atmosphere and re-enter over its target at such speed that no defence would be possible. When the warhead struck the ground, the damage was devastating. And finally there was the lesser known V-3. This was a gun over 400 feet long which would fire finned projectiles with 300 lbs of high explosive over a distance of 100 miles. Two batteries, each with twenty-five guns, were being built to the south of Calais, their shafts all targeted on London. This was known as 'the London Gun'.

Hitler's plan was to have these new weapons ready swiftly so that the Allied invasion of northern France could be defeated before it ever set sail. The flying bombs, which were by now in mass production, the high altitude rockets, which could not be intercepted, and the London Guns, which would be firing once every six seconds, would – the Germans hoped – reduce London to rubble and annihilate the invasion force known to be gathering in the south-east of England.

For the Allies, the invasion preparations were becoming a race against time. But the building of the concrete caissons for the floating harbours was proving difficult and was slipping behind schedule. At one site near Portsmouth, a caisson collapsed causing many casualties. To step up production, more work was transferred to London sites. But a tremendous shortage of labour was developing in the capital. To overcome this, building workers and dockers from all corners of the country were directed to work in London and large numbers of Irish labourers were recruited, including Tom Feeney from Galway:

> The Ministry of Labour sent recruiting officers over and there were thousands of young men like me who were looking for adventure and wanted to do their bit for the war effort. I was a cabinet-maker by trade and my job was to help build the basic wooden structure of the Mulberrys which they filled in with concrete. It was a real challenge, we'd never done anything like it before, but we got the hang of it in no time.

The great array of equipment needed was taking time to develop and build. The invasion of France could not be rushed and the date was set for May 1944. In the meantime, the Allies simply had to try to knock out Hitler's secret weapons. The intelligence services had long been tracking the development of the V-1 flying bomb and the V-2 rocket and had felt that they had successfully disrupted both by bombing the testing site at Peenemunde. In response to the new information about the launching ramps in northern France, the British and American air forces mounted an intensive bombing campaign to destroy them. As for the London Gun, British Intelligence never knew anything about it. By early in 1944, the Allies consequently believed that the threat had been countered.

By now, the invasion preparations in the capital were also beginning to bear fruit. Fords at Dagenham had developed an invaluable waterproofing compound made of red putty. London Transport's Acton works had converted tanks to operate in water 10 feet deep. A Thames-side submarine cable company had tested strong but flexible piping on the floor of the Thames for use in the Pluto project. The furniture makers in north London were busy expanding their range of military products. Alongside Mosquito planes, there were troop-carrying gliders specially adapted for landing on grassland behind the German lines on the French coast, assault dinghies and wooden pontoons for the floating roadway.

In the London docks, the newly converted dry docks were flooded and the first batch of half-completed caissons for the Mulberry harbour were floated out and round to the remaining 'wet' docks for finishing off. Tom Feeney recalls: 'They ended up as high as a block of flats, thousands of tons of concrete and steel. We'd never seen anything like it and we wondered if it would ever float. I remember the day they dug a canal to take the Mulberry out by tug into the Thames. And when the tide came up the canal we all watched secretly fearing it might sink, then as the water got higher and higher, it started floating and everyone started clapping and cheering.'

Meanwhile, Hitler was beginning to get uneasy. The German troops in Italy were coming under increasing pressure from the Allies advancing from the south. And on the Eastern Front the Soviets were pushing the German forces back through the Ukraine. Hitler heard reports that the Allied invasion plans were well under way. He wanted to disrupt these preparations but his secret V-weapons were not yet ready, partly because the Allied bombing missions had caused disruption and partly because of some remaining technical problems. So he turned to conventional bombing and on 21 January, he ordered every serviceable aircraft in the West to attack London.

The raid was not a success – only thirty tons of the high explosive carried by the Luftwaffe hit their targets. The attack was renewed in February, when several raids by the Luftwaffe brought death and destruction back to the capital. The raids were christened the 'baby blitz' – but they were nothing like the blitz itself in terms of the damage they inflicted. Moreover, the improved defences of London were soon beginning to take their toll on the Luftwaffe. The German counter-offensive began to fade and, after a few more attacks, ended at the end of March.

The preparations for Operation Overlord in London and on the south coast were now reaching their climax. All along the Thames, the river banks were bristling with concrete barges and with converted Thames barges, their sterns cut off and replaced with ramps ready for the landings. And the first batch of caissons for the Mulberry harbour were completed. These massive concrete units formed a truly curious sight to Londoners as they floated out of the docks and down the river. Though most people in the capital guessed that the moment of invasion was near, few people outside the docks knew of the floating harbours which had been kept a close secret by the project's workers. Indeed, precautions were taken to ensure that information about the D-day preparations were not leaked to German intelligence. Tom Feeney remembers the importance placed on secrecy at the time:

> We all knew what we were doing was part of the invasion plan but they tried to keep it secret outside the East End. There were noticed posted up everywhere saying 'DANGEROUS TALK COSTS LIVES'. We, the Irish, were banned from going home so that we wouldn't go out and boast about what we were doing, and let the secret out and get back to Germany. And all the letters home were opened and censored as well, to stop any secrets getting out; many was the letter I sent home which had 'opened by the censor' marked on it.

The caissons were then towed round to the Solent, waiting for the rest of the units, still behind schedule, to be finished. For separate military reasons, the date of the invasion – D-day, as it was called – had to be put back from May to June. The harbours were frantically finished. All the preparations were ready.

In the last weeks of May and early June, the tension began to mount as

A poignant scene at Euston Station in the spring of 1944 as D-day approaches and London fills up with troops soon to do battle on the beaches of Normandy

thousands of troops passed through the capital on their way to the south coast. Many were temporarily housed in makeshift military camps erected on the bombed-out wilderness which was once Canning Town and Silvertown or on London's football grounds, for example West Ham's Upton Park. Six divisions gathered in the London docks waiting for embarkation. On Tuesday, 6 June 1944, hundreds of ships set off down the Thames. As they rounded the coast, they joined thousands more vessels and tugs leaving from the south coast ports. The greatest amphibious assault in history was underway. Very early that morning, the first troops had landed on the beaches of Normandy. This was D-day.

These landings were swiftly followed up by a massive surge of back-up troops. On the next day, the enormous caissons of the two Mulberry harbours were towed from the south coast over to Normandy, one for the British landing areas and one for the American. Once in position, their valves were opened, water flooded in and these great concrete structures sank. The harbour walls had finally completed their historic journey from the docks of the Thames to the rough waters off the coast of Normandy. In the lee of the new harbours, ships could already move in to unload. At the same time, the floating piers and the floating roadways were locked into the seaborne system. Off came tanks, trucks, jeeps, field guns, and eventually a daily delivery of 9,000 tons of equipment and supplies. Meanwhile, the great Pluto pipeline began to be laid, eventually to carry a million gallons of petrol a day to the front line. In the battle which immediately followed D-day more than 3,000 Allied troops were killed, and double that number injured. Two weeks later fierce Channel gales were to wreck the Mulberry harbour, used by the U.S. forces off Omaha Beach, and damage the British Mulberry off Arromanches. But by this time the invasion force had successfully landed on the beaches of Normandy and begun to penetrate the German defence lines. The Allied invasion of France was going well.

For Londoners, the tension and pressure of the last few months, the hard work of the productions drives over the past three years, the sacrifices of the war, all seemed worthwhile. The Allies were on the road to victory. Londoners' spirits had never been higher – for no one suspected that a terrible shock was in store for them.

5

THE FINAL TERROR

Previous pages: One of the victims of the Aldwych doodlebug disaster, 30 June 1944. The doodlebugs, or pilotless planes, brought a final wave of terror to London. They were launched towards the capital from just across the Channel, and were designed to explode on impact

Below: Death on the streets after the Aldwych doodlebug disaster. The explosive power of these flying bombs brought a new kind of devastation to London

Around sunrise on Tuesday, 13 June 1944 a strange machine-like noise could be heard travelling through the sky above London. Those who were awake thought it sounded like an old motor bike, a powerful sawmill or a huge clockwork toy. They weren't particularly disturbed, for Londoners had gone to bed that night in a more calm and confident mood than on almost any night since the war had begun. They had read in the papers of the successful D-day landings and looked forward to a swift victory as the Allied forces advanced through German-held territory. It was now three years since the blitz had ended and, despite sporadic air attacks, it seemed as if London's days in the front line were over. Most Londoners were blissfully unaware that they were about to become the target for a new terror weapon, the V-1, a pilotless plane designed to explode on impact, launched by the Luftwaffe from just across the Channel.

The first missile arrived at 4.25 a.m., shattering the peace of Grove Road in the heart of Bow. The 'Bow bomb' was in fact just one of ten mis-

siles – shortly to become known as flying bombs or doodlebugs – which
had been hurled from their camouflaged catapult bases in northern
France. Of these, five crashed almost at once, one plummeted into the
Channel, and three fell to earth in Kent causing little damage. But even
though only one flying bomb landed on its target, it was quite devastating
in its effects. It was a sign of what was to come, for it marked the beginning of a new major air offensive on London that was to have an enormous impact on life in the capital. The 'strike' rate of the flying bombs
increased swiftly as the Germans added the final touches to the program-
ming and launching of their missiles. Within three days, the flying bombs
were reaching Greater London at the rate of seventy-three a day.

The missiles brought a new sort of devastation to London. Whereas
during the blitz the destruction had been caused largely by incendiary
bombs and fire, now it resulted more or less completely from bomb blast.
The greater explosive power of the bomb, combined with the lack of
warning of its arrival, resulted in a gruesome fate for those in the
immediate vicinity of the point of impact. The warheads were of such
force that they damaged houses and shattered windows within a quarter
of a mile radius. The direct blast of the explosion hurled people against
obstacles, crashed them into walls and in the most serious cases literally
ripped them apart. Spears of flying glass lacerated people, sometimes
causing serious injuries, such as blindness. Others were hurt by objects
like flying rubble or pieces of wood which struck them heavy blows or

Elsie Huntley, her son Derek and baby Roy, photographed a few weeks before a doodlebug blast buried them in a street shelter in Mitcham, killing Derek

pierced them like arrows. Those who were inside their home, work place or street shelter when the missile struck, were likely to be buried alive if they were within fifty yards of the explosion. In one early doodlebug raid in south London, Elsie Huntley, her nine-year-old son Derek and her baby Roy huddled together with neighbours in the concrete street shelter opposite their home in Mitcham:

It was the most terrible night we knew. We had a lot of bombing all night long. They were coming over all night, warnings coming and going. And then in the morning it had eased off quite a bit and I suggested I go in and make a cup of tea. Anyway, I went in the house to make the tea, I'd got the baby with me, he was nearly two. My son, who was nine, came running in and said, 'Mummy, there's one coming over.' So I said, 'You run over the shelter and get into your bed and I'll come in.' So I came in quickly and I hadn't been in there a few minutes when we heard the noise stop. Well, we knew when it stopped something was going to happen and then, bang, everything went dark. I leant over my baby and we were all screaming; I could hear my neighbours screaming, I was screaming, the baby was screaming. So I tried to ease myself away so that the baby could breathe, because everything was crushing us. All the concrete was on top of us. And then I just thought, 'Oh God, what's happened, please help me, get me out.'

It seemed ages, but I think it was only a few minutes when I heard above me movements and voices, and I'm saying, 'Please help me, please help me'. Gradually I managed to push my arm out and somebody held my hand and was saying, 'Hold on lady, hold on.' And I said, 'I've got a baby, got a baby in my arms,' and then they pulled my baby out and got me out.

We were all put in an ambulance and taken to hospital. I was laid on a bed in a casualty ward and when somebody brought the baby round saying 'Whose baby is this?' And I said 'It's my baby.' In the morning they said to me that my other son Derek had been killed outright. And all the women neighbours were killed as well.

To avoid any panic, and to prevent German intelligence from discovering what damage the V-1 was wreaking, Herbert Morrison, the Minister for Home Security, at first censored any reference to the flying bombs. Many of those who had seen or heard the first missiles believed they were German raiders shot down over London. But when the intensity of the attack increased concealment was no longer possible; the people of London needed to be told something of what was happening to them so that new precautions could be taken. On 16 June Herbert Morrison announced that London was under attack by pilotless planes. He still insisted, however, that the true extent of the destructive power of the flying bomb be covered up.

In fact, Londoners have still not been told the whole truth about what really happened in this final attack on the capital. The scale of devastation and demoralization caused by the flying bombs was hushed up at the time in order to maintain morale. The secrets of London's ordeal were then locked away in government files. Now that these records have been opened to the public, they reveal that during the last nine months of the war London and its inhabitants faced a supreme challenge.

This challenge came when Londoners were ill-equipped to face renewed suffering. They were tired and exhausted from five long years of war. Moreover, most people had believed that the landings in France would bring more or less instant victory. But instead there was a return to the anxiety of the blitz. The disappointed expectations made the new hardship more difficult to bear. To most Londoners it seemed inconceivable that the Allies, with their overwhelming strength, could not destroy a few hundred missile sites just across the Channel now that they had invaded France. Many blamed the government; Morrison, once the hero of Londoners, found himself booed as he visited bomb-damaged areas. The great spirit of solidarity and faith in the state, which had been generated during the blitz and sustained till D-day, was beginning to dissipate.

The damaging and demoralizing effects of the flying bombs were quickly seized upon by the German propaganda machine – and then much exaggerated. Fictitious newspaper reports spoke of thousands lying dead in the streets, many more fleeing the capital for their lives, and civilian life grinding to a standstill. One of the principal aims of the flying bomb attack was to boost German morale. Since 1942 one German city after another – and in particular Berlin – had been subjected to saturation bombing by the British and American air forces. Almost all the victims had been civilians. Indeed the Allies' deliberate aim – though this had not been publicly admitted – was to break German morale by 'de-housing' the population of the industrial cities as well as destroying the factories where they worked. The results were far worse than anything that London had ever experienced. The bombing of Hamburg in July 1943, for example, created a mammoth fire-storm which burned for several days and killed over 50,000. Now London was to take the brunt of an attack that was provoked primarily by a German desire for retribution. The Reich christened the flying bomb Vergeltungswaffe, vengeance weapon.

London was the principal target of these V-1s. Early in 1944 Hitler spent many hours with Goebbels drawing squares on a map of London and working out how many people each missile might kill. When the attacks had begun, he ordered that no flying bombs be used against any other target than London. But, except in his wilder moments, Hitler didn't seriously believe that this attack on London was a way of defeating Britain. He simply wanted to kill indiscriminately as many Londoners as possible and perhaps thereby stave off defeat a little longer. 'You can only smash terror with terror' Hitler had declared when giving priority to V-weapon production.

The final bombing campaign brought a whole new dimension to the idea that civilians were legitimate military targets. From the beginning of the blitz it was clear that citizens were seen by both sides as fair game for the bomber. But what happened in the last year of the war was that the scale of attacks on civilians was escalating while their military significance was diminishing. Any gentlemanly code of conduct or compassion which had previously spared civilians – at least in theory – was now disappearing. When combined with the new technological developments in the weaponry of death it meant that the nightmare of mass extermination envisaged by military experts at the beginning of the war was now becoming reality.

British Intelligence had long suspected that Germany was about to use new secret weapons to attack London. However, the government mistakenly believed that the heavy Allied bombing raids during the winter of 1943-44 had all but knocked out the launching sites and disrupted the missile production programme. As a result of this false confidence, the defences of London were scaled down; the number of guns protecting the capital was almost halved. But suddenly London was again under attack.

How would Londoners stand up to the new bombardment? The government required an urgent answer to this question. To discover how Londoners were reacting ministers looked to the Home Intelligence reports which monitored public opinion in the capital. The reports must have made disturbing reading. They noted a high level of strain, and weariness, strong criticism of government inaction, and a general feeling that this new onslaught was harder to bear than the blitz. In some parts of London they reported a 'general rush to the shelters when a bomb is heard and men are said to show little sign of the women and children first spirit'. Odette Lesley has a vivid memory of this new panic that gripped the capital. She had been forced to give up her war work because of physical exhaustion, and was now making handbags in central London, 'I can still remember my horror and disgust at seeing grown men avidly pushing women and children aside to get down into Warren Street tube station when the doodlebugs were coming over. I was actually shoved out of the way myself once or twice. People's nerves had gone, their nerves were shot to pieces.'

The official fear of a 'deep shelter mentality' developing amongst tube shelterers – which had proved groundless during the blitz – now seemed to be coming true. Some Londoners, especially those with young children, lived in the tubes day and night, refusing to leave until ejected by the police so that the shelters could be cleaned. People felt that the war was nearly over and did not want to be killed by one of the last bombs. Whereas in 1940 the mood had, in part, been one of self-sacrifice, now it was more exclusively self-preservation to get through to the end. Most civilians secretly felt, or even openly said, that the war should have been won by now anyway.

Within days, the flying bomb raids had created intense feelings of strain and anxiety. At the same time, the old spirit of cooperation and communality began to be replaced by a new sort of individualism. These changes resulted from a whole constellation of factors which had not been present during the blitz.

First, there was the lack of warning of imminent disaster. One moment, people would be going about their normal business – walking to school, doing the housework, shopping, working in the office – and the next they could be seconds away from death. The flying bombs, which by the end of June were hitting London at the rate of about a hundred a day, left the old air raid warning system – which had worked quite well during the blitz –

practically redundant. The flying bombs were so small and fast that they sometimes managed to avoid radar detection: as a result there was no air raid warning or the warning was sounded too late for families to find shelter. At other times, the alert went so frequently that people found it difficult to remember if an alert was in force or not. To get any work done at all, many stayed where they were so they could continue working and instead listened for the flying bomb. This could be a nerve-wracking business. There would be a distant hum rising to a raucous rattle which would either disappear into the distance or suddenly stop. It was the interval between when the engine cut out and the explosion which was the most terrifying. If the noise seemed to stop directly above them people would dive for cover, flinging themselves on the floor, under tables or in doorways. This interval lasted only twelve seconds but seemed interminable. This combination of an ever-present possibility of death and destruction, and the shortness of the warning, created a feeling

A doodlebug framed by the spire of the High Court building, plummets to earth and explodes in the Drury Lane area of Covent Garden, 6 July 1944

This was one of the 2,350 V-1s to land on London during the summer of that year, killing more than 5,000 civilians and seriously injuring 15,000 more

A flying bomb scores a direct hit on the Palace Engineering Works, Lambeth Road

The London Fire Brigade Headquarters on the Albert Embankment is only 300 yards away and firemen arrive at the scene within minutes. Together with rescue workers and passers-by, they help to extricate survivors

The flying bombs brought the ever present possibility of death to Londoners, for they arrived at any moment of the day or night, usually heralded by little or no air raid warning

of isolation. As the flying bombs could come any moment day or night, there was no specific period when people would come together to shelter, yet when destruction was near there wasn't time to draw strength from one another.

Charlie Draper, now working repairing bomb-damaged buildings in south London, found the constant danger a terrible strain:

> You never knew when one was going to get you. There were several occasions I had near misses. One was when I was blown off a motorbike when a fly bomb dropped in Dulwich. On another occasion I was buried for five hours in a market in East Lane and was dug out. And another occasion, when I was at Penge, a fly bomb came over. We heard the engine stop and we all rushed into this ice box in the fishmongers, and it dropped just over the back of the shop and the door slammed so hard that when we got out of there we all had gone slightly deaf. I think at that time I was more or less knackered and that did me in. So I went in the shop next door, got a couple of pies, put them in my tool bag, collected my tools together and jumped on a bus and went off to the Chislehurst caves. I didn't actually go into the caves, I lay down in a field opposite and I just slept for about seven hours, so I must have been on the edge of collapse.

Second, the robotic and depersonalized nature of the flying bombs fuelled many irrational fears. The most common was that the doodlebugs were programmed to reach certain specific targets and had the power to seek them out and pursue them. This was, in fact, far beyond the capabilities of the V-1s but such fears seemed to be given substance by the remarkable frequency with which the bombs scored direct hits on hospitals in London. More than a hundred were hit by doodlebugs, amongst them St Mary Abbotts in Kensington, Mile End, Lambeth and St Olave's. Some people believed that the weapons had been targetted against the sick and the helpless. The whole nature of these pilotless machines was like something out of a science fiction story. The thought of being killed by a robot was for many much more unnerving than being bombed by a pilot, who might himself be shot down and killed in the process, as Odette Lesley makes clear:

> The doodlebugs were so much more terrifying than anything that had come along up till that time because they were supernatural, they were uncanny, they were almost science fiction. It was so awful to think about this destructive thing up there, full of explosive, with this awful flame coming out, and nobody in it. You accepted a plane with a man in it, you couldn't accept something that was automatic. It was this that struck psychologically at us in such a way that it destroyed our nerves, it destroyed any sort of calm that we'd worked out through the war. We could not accept this.

Another key factor leading to widespread demoralization was the new pattern of attacks. Conventional air attacks had tended to concentrate on built-up areas and industrial zones but, because the flying bombs could not be targetted in the same way, leafy suburbs now found themselves in the front line. Over half of the flying bombs rained down on the suburbs of south London, with Croydon, Lewisham and Wandsworth (in that order) worst hit. Even if the bombs did not actually fall, the residents had the unnerving experience of watching processions of doodlebugs pass overhead on their way to central London.

This new geography of the bombing brought into the front line the suburban housewife, whom Home Intelligence reported as being particularly upset by the new attacks. Many woman strained to hear the bombs as they went about their daily chores, only to discover that the domestic sounds of running taps, sizzling food and buzzing vacuum cleaners could easily be confused with approaching flying bombs or, even worse, could make the real thing inaudible. They did not have the benefit of roof observers to warn them of impending danger as did factories and department stores. These suburban housewives often spent all day by themselves or with their young children, and did not have the support or the camaraderie which, during the blitz, had given strength to the families then in the forefront of the attack. The result of all this strain was that some of these tired housewives were on the verge of nervous breakdowns, unable to keep going for much longer. Gladys Strelitz had now moved back from Caversham where she was evacuated, and was living with her children in Ilford, in Essex:

> It was dreadful because we had a big room, with a big open window space, and we'd look out and see this flaming sword coming right over, and it always appeared as if it was coming for us. And we would have to fall on the floor, lie under the table, and wait for the crash that would come. We knew every minute that it might be our last. It was intolerable, it really was. And in the end it had its effect on me because I started sleep-walking, and I'd have to be helped down the stairs, and I knew I couldn't carry on much longer, that something would have to be done about it. All the tablets the doctor was giving me weren't helping me a little bit, so I ended up with nervous exhaustion.

In addition, the post-blitz lull in bombings had resulted in a gradual winding down of the whole civil defence network. The great demand for recruits in the forces and for war production had led to the transfer of tens of thousands of men and women away from civil defence work. Morrison, partly to compensate for this reduction in public provision, distributed thousands more of his indoor table shelters known as 'Morrison's', which had originally been developed during the blitz to give Londoners greater protection in their own homes. However, although these strong and well designed shelters offered excellent protection against flying glass and masonry, they helped to increase the isolation of the individual family and in particular the housewife, who was now likely to remain in her house when a raid was on.

Underlying the new mood of anxiety and despondency that had

emerged was a deep physical and mental weariness with the war. One of the key factors contributing to this tiredness was the long-term effects of rationing – a necessary and, to begin with, a popular strategy. The Ministry of Food, with its Kitchen Front publicity campaign, had raised public awareness of what were 'healthy foods'; indeed improvements in some people's diets had resulted. However, most people were becoming fed up with their food. Many cherished items like fresh eggs, oranges and onions had virtually disappeared. New foods considered repugnant by many, like whale meat, cat fish or pig's brains, had found their way onto people's dinner plates. The strict rationing of basic items like meat, butter, bacon and cheese had for many people taken much of the pleasure out of eating. People were bored with carrot marmalade, dried eggs, and 'Woolton' vegetable pie, made out of a mixture of potato, swede, cauliflower and carrots.

By 1944, when the novelty had worn off, people desperately wanted to return to the foods they had once enjoyed. More important, housewives were exhausted by the constant scrimping and saving, the queueing for hours outside fishmongers and greengrocers, and the struggle to make a wholesome, filling meal from a few ingredients. And when the effort became too much or the queues too long, then they and their families went hungry. Gladys Strelitz kept going for the sake of her children:

> There was all this lining up for food. A neighbour might say, 'Yes, they've got sausages down the road,' and you'd rush out, line up for an hour, two hours, and when you got to the counter, all they'd have was whale meat sausages. Take them home and while you were cooking them, these sausages were so revolting they actually smelt of fish. Well, we ate them in front of the children to prove that they were lovely, but they weren't really. The children would say, 'No, we don't want those, Mummy', so then we would mix up swede with them to take the taste away, and we'd see the tears running down their cheeks. But we knew the children had to be fed and they couldn't go hungry. We couldn't put 'em to bed hungry. So, day after day we kept on like this. There was nothing else.

The rationing of clothes was also by now biting severely into people's living standards. Since the spring of 1942, the basic clothing ration had been spartan but the real impact of this only came after two or three years. By then, rationed clothes had worn out before enough points had been accumulated on the rationing system to buy replacements. The Make Do And Mend campaign and the introduction of better quality utility clothes had improved the situation a little but, even so, many suits, overcoats and dresses had a very frayed and tattered look. This was particularly depressing for younger people, many of whom wanted to cultivate a fashionable look. In desperation young women painted imitation stocking seams in their legs to give the impression they were wearing nylons. Middle-class families usually fared best because they had a stock of good quality clothes before rationing had begun. Poorer families – although they were used to hand-me-downs – found it very difficult to get by. Home Intelligence reported considerable anger at the inadequacy of the clothes rations.

The rationing of household items could be equally demoralizing. Again, the effect was cumulative, peaking in 1944 and 1945 when more and more everyday things had broken or were worn out. Toilet paper had become scarce – most made do with the traditional working-class substitute of ripped-up newspapers, though even this was in short supply as the daily newspaper was now only four pages long. There was a shortage of millions of pieces of crockery and some families were forced to drink from jam jars as the poorest had done in the 1930s. Furniture was rigidly rationed and even bombed-out families were allowed only a few essential pieces to set up their new homes. As furniture became more and more threadbare, dyed flour sacks and sugar bags were commonly used for covers and cushions. Cots were in very short supply by the end of the war and pregnant women were advised to make one out of an old drawer, by padding it with newspaper and then lining it with an old nightdress. It was very difficult to obtain everyday items like saucepans, kettles, alarm clocks, bedding, toothbrushes, paint and carpets. Cutlery was difficult to replace and much was pilfered from canteens. By 1944 the number of knives, forks, and spoons that were disappearing each year from the canteens run by the London Transport Passenger Board had risen astronomically to more than sixty thousand.

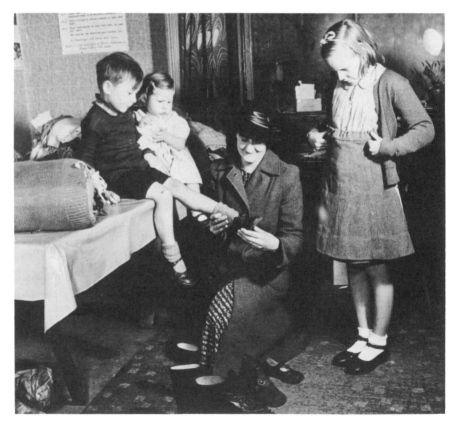

The W.V.S. Childrens' Clothing Exchange at Gypsy Hill, Norwood, 1944. By this time many mothers were exhausted by the constant scrimping and saving that rationing involved: inadequate childrens' clothing was a frequent complaint among working-class women

The growing disillusionment with rationing, and the growing desire of people to obtain more than their fair share, helped to fuel a substantial increase in crime in the last years of the war. In 1938, 10 in every 1,000 people in London were committing crimes – by 1944 it had risen to a peak of 15, representing a fifty per cent increase. An enormous amount of crime, moreover, went unrecorded and undetected because of the black-out and the depletion of the police force during the war.

Behind the increase in crime in the capital lay the insatiable demand of the black market. There was an especially big demand for everyday rationed items like meat, clothing and cigarettes. Professional criminals in London moved away from their traditional pursuits such as stealing from well-to-do houses, and started hijacking lorries loaded with food and clo-thing, and raiding warehouses. There was a boom in pilfering from work places – dockers, warehousemen and those involved in the transporta-tion of goods often had the richest pickings – and most of this stolen prop-erty found its way onto the black market. Ordinary civilians increasingly dabbled in crime both as pilferers and purchasers of stolen goods. They bought the goods 'under the counter,' without any rationing coupons exchanging hands, in shops and markets or from 'spivs' who would fix up deals in pubs.

The main beneficiaries of the black market were probably the middle classes, simply by virtue of their greater purchasing power. They particu-larly wanted meat and eggs, which could be obtained, at a price, through markets like Romford and Chelmsford in Essex, where local farmers brought their goods to sell at a high price on the black market. But there was also a considerable working-class demand for illicit food and clo-thing: many were better paid during the war than they had ever been, and were unable to spend their money on what they considered essential items.

However, although the black market understandably gave a boost to some families, enabling them to enjoy little luxuries that would otherwise have been denied them, on a deeper level it was extremely divisive and depressing. Its growth and its increasing visibility encouraged the view that sacrifices were not being equally shared and that some people weren't pulling together anymore, they were just looking after 'number one' – as Odette Lesley remembers:

The black market was everywhere. You'd go into your grocer's and he'd say, 'Got some peaches', or 'Got some corned beef today', or whatever was rationed or unavailable. You'd make an offer as to what you'd pay for it; it was always above the normal price. You could buy coupons for food or clothing off workmates, or perhaps from spivs in pubs. The whole thing was really causing a terrible lot of bad feeling and resentment. If you did an under-the-counter deal, you wouldn't tell anyone who wasn't a close friend because you might get lynched. In factories and offices people were getting very aggressive about it. You'd hear 'It's not bleedin' right', 'So and so's got this and that'. Often it was the green eye of jealousy.

Also, there was a widespread belief amongst the working classes that the better off were continuing to enjoy the fruits of the good life via the black market. This heightened feeling that the rich were anyway getting a better deal by finding legal ways around the rationing laws. For example, though a five-shilling maximum had been placed on restaurant meals in 1942, the rich continued to run up bills of several pounds in exclusive West End restaurants. The Communist Party began a crusade against such inequality of sacrifice during 1944 and 1945 which attracted considerable support from poorer people in places like Stepney and Poplar.

The government was painfully aware of this increasing tension and tiredness in the capital. In addition, it was becoming more and more concerned with the damage inflicted by the doodlebugs. After two weeks of flying-bomb attacks London had suffered almost as much damage as during the same period at the beginning of the blitz. About 1,600 had been killed, about 10,000 were injured, half of them seriously, and over 200,000 houses had been damaged.

Only the end walls are left standing in Rectory Road, Stoke Newington, after a hit from a doodlebug. During the first two weeks of the flying bomb attacks over 200,000 houses in the capital were damaged or destroyed

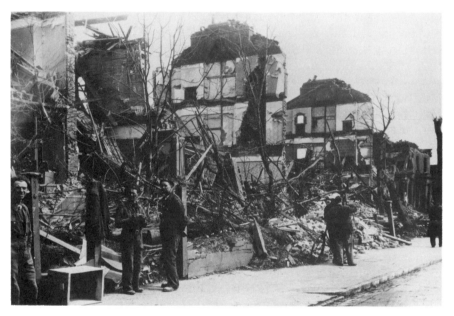

When the war cabinet met on 27 June opinion was unanimous that the capital faced a crisis. Morrison saw the new attacks as a real threat to Allied victory. He argued that 'after five years of war the civil population were not as capable of standing the strains of air attacks as they had been during the winter of 1940-41. I will do everything to hold up their courage and spirit – but there is a limit and the limit will come'. Initiatives to avert this impending crisis were taken on a number of different fronts.

An official evacuation scheme was quickly put into operation. From the first days of the flying-bomb attacks, the better off had privately evacuated themselves and their families, piling their possessions into taxis and driving to country retreats. But for the majority this was too costly. The government evacuation schemes, introduced in early July, led to almost 500,000 mothers, expectant mothers and children being billeted

Firemen lend a hand in the evacuation of mothers and children from St Pancras Station, 14 July 1944. The new evacuation schemes to get Londoners away from the doodlebug danger led to a million people leaving the capital by the end of the summer

on strangers in the country. Another 500,000 – including elderly people and homeless families – left London as 'aided evacuees': they made their own arrangements but were given free railway warrants and billeting certificates entitling them to a weekly allowance. By the end of August the population of London had dropped by more than 1,000,000.

This new exodus greatly improved the conditions for those who remained in London. The shelters immediately became less crowded and verminous. Conditions improved still further in early July when the government opened eight new purpose-built deep shelters, four on the north bank of the Thames at Chancery Lane, Goodge Street, Camden Town and Belsize Park, and four on the south, at Stockwell, Clapham North, Clapham South and Clapham Common. Each of them was 100 feet underground and contained 8,000 bunks as well as canteen and hospital facilities. Those lucky enough to get tickets felt like the aristocrats of the shelter world. In addition, Londoners found that with fewer mouths to feed in the capital there was more food available for each person than at any time since the war began.

All this helped Londoners to cope with the effects of the flying bombs. But the most important task for the government was to try to stop the bombs actually landing on the capital. Here British Intelligence played a key role. The German military chiefs had no knowledge of what targets the bombs were hitting, despite their propaganda claiming that the new offensive had brought London to its knees. The Germans relied on a handful of secret agents that they had sent to Britain during the war to provide them with this information. But in fact these agents were all captured and were being used to feed back phoney information. When flying bombs landed on central London, these agents reported that they had overshot their mark and hit the countryside to the north. They also reported that no flying bombs had landed south of the Thames, despite the fact that around three-quarters of the bombs had fallen in this area. In response to this 'information', the German crews re-adjusted the flying bombs' guidance mechanisms believing that the bombs were now more

accurately aimed at their target of central London. In fact, these adjustments meant that the programmed point of impact moved from Tower
Bridge to Dulwich, five miles to the south. This in turn meant that many
bombs did little damage, landing in the countryside to the south of London and that most northern, central and even inner southern suburbs
were spectacularly better off. They experienced a dramatic reduction in
the frequency of bombing. But the plan also meant an increased burden of
bombings for areas like Croydon, Bromley, Bexley and Orpington. As
these outer areas were much less densely populated than the inner areas,
each incident caused on average far fewer casualties. But, nevertheless,
for those that lived in the south London suburbs, the risk of death was
increased. This was the price that had to be paid.

Equally important in protecting London from the flying-bomb attacks
were four lines of defence that were rapidly assembled in late June and
early July. First, there were several squadrons of Hawker Tempests, Spitfires and other fighters patrolling the Channel twenty miles off-shore between Dover and Beachy Head. The fighter pilots chased the flying
bombs and attempted to shoot them down in mid-air. The next line of
defence was thousands of anti-aircraft guns – including those which had
once been in London – placed on the coast along a fifty-mile stretch
behind the patrolling aircraft. The ack ack units had by this stage been
much improved with rocket projectors, radar guidance for the guns and
'proximity' fuses on the shells, which meant that the shells exploded not
only when they hit their target but also when they were near. Behind the
guns were more fighters to deal with any missiles which got through the
gun belt. Finally, along the North Downs, floated an armada of barrage
balloons, which by mid-July numbered 1,750. To begin with, lack of
experience in dealing with the flying bombs meant that most passed
through the defence system intact. But by the end of July the anti-aircraft

Houses are blown over and a huge crater appears in Staveley Road, Chiswick, after the first V-2 rocket lands on London, 8 September 1944. All information about the new rocket attacks was censored for two months

gunners and the R.A.F. pilots were having considerable success in shooting them down. Between mid-June and early September a total of 3,916 bombs – just over a half of all those directed at London – were blown up. The fighters brought down 1,942, the guns 1,730 and the balloons 244. By then, however, the flying bombs had killed nearly 5,781 people and severely injured 15,530 more.

Renewed Allied air attacks on the missile bases in northern France also met with much success in restricting the number of flying bombs launched towards London. By early August, twenty-five doodlebugs were landing on the capital each day compared to one hundred a month earlier. By the end of August this had shrunk to four or five. This dramatic reduction was ultimately due to the abandonment of launching sites in the face of the Allied advance. Military chiefs announced that practically all launching areas had been captured. And as they pushed forward, the Allied troops stumbled across Germany's only truly secret weapon – the V-3, known as the London Gun. Constant damage by Allied air attacks and a lack of technical expertise amongst the German military meant that this new weapon was still not ready for use. The London Gun was captured before it ever fired a shot.

On 5 September victory fever spread around London, with flag-waving celebrations in the streets as rumours spread that the bombings were all over. The prevailing euphoria even infected ministers, and on 7 September Herbert Morrison ordered an end to the evacuation of London. Later that day Duncan Sandys, the junior minister in charge of the V-bomb problem, told a press conference that 'except possibly for a few last shots the Battle of London is over'. Many Londoners, hearing this news, considered the war to be virtually won and thousands of evacuated families flooded back into the capital.

The celebrations were premature. The next day, on the evening of 8 September, a mysterious explosion was heard all over London. It was immediately followed by a second explosion. Chiswick to the west and Epping in Essex to the east were the areas affected. After this the strange explosions continued and increased, so that by the end of October an average of four a day were heard in London. And all the time the return of evacuees into the capital continued, most of them oblivious to the new danger that now faced them. The government had ordered a total censorship on any reference to the true nature of these explosions – a barrage of German rockets was hitting the capital. Dore Silverman was one of a team of press censors who worked round the clock at the M.O.I. headquarters in Senate House, combing through 'sensitive' copy from editors, taking out any reference to rocket damage:

We had to stop the knowledge of their arrival being circulated, first, so as not to inform the Germans that they had landed in any particular area, but more important, there was the question of morale of the civilian population, because these were devastating in their effect. One rocket could demolish a whole street in a working-class area. There was no defence against them. And there was no warning that they were on their way and you could not take any shelter of any kind, because you had not even five seconds' notice.

But soon the mysterious bangs had become so common that many people were frightened and wild rumours circulated as to what they might be. Some said they were exploding gas mains, others thought that German paratroopers were blowing up key installations.

The explosions were not as frequent as those during the blitz or the flying-bomb attack, but what was really causing the alarm was their apparent size. Each one was heralded by a double bang so loud that even at ten miles away it sounded close by. Immediately afterwards there was a reddish flash and a large plume of black smoke rose into the sky. At the point of impact, it was clear that these explosions were the result of a new and yet more powerful type of bomb. There would be a crater, sometimes as much as fifty feet wide and ten feet deep. In the immediate vicinity a whole row of perhaps thirty terraced houses would be virtually razed to the ground. Suburban streets suddenly took on the appearance of battlefields with clouds of dust, masses of rubble and the dead and injured lying everywhere, some with dismembered limbs, and all covered in blood. Many close to the explosions who survived were permanently blinded. An earthquake effect reverberated causing yet more damage: a quarter of a mile away, windows smashed, roofs caved in and washbasins cracked; a few miles away, the earth tremor was such that floorboards shuddered, window frames shook and clouds of soot were blown out of fireplaces into living rooms. Charlie Draper, whose job it was to help patch up bomb-damaged buildings in the Peckham area, remembered the enormity of the rocket damage and the demoralization it caused:

> It was a lot worse than what the doodlebugs did. It would take out a row of houses or a block of flats; the complete block would just disappear. And then, say, another hundred yards away the walls were caved in, party-walls were gone, roofs blown off, the structure was in a terrible state. They were irreparable. They just pulled them down, dangerous structures. We patched up the ones further away.
>
> In some of the houses we went in we'd see some of the people that were there when it happened. They might have been in their shelter, then come out in the morning and found the house half gone. They were upset and cracking up and saying, 'Oh, this is the sixth time this has happened. You know, I don't think I'll ever start again. I've had enough.' When we were at the rocket sites, it was terrible. They were digging people out for days after, and finding bodies on roofs all the way around the area.

British Intelligence had known about the development of the V-2, a new type of 'rocket' bomb, since 1943 but had mistakenly believed that Allied air attacks in that year and 1944 had all but destroyed the rocket production process and the launching pads. They were unaware of the existence of a major rocket assembly line – run by a slave army of prisoners from concentration camps – deep in the Hartz mountains outside Nord-hausen. While the Allies advanced towards Germany and the R.A.F. continued to pound German cities, these V-2 rockets provided Hitler and his military chiefs with their last chance for attack and revenge. London was the largest, closest and most obvious target for the new revenge weapon. The legitimacy of mass civilian annihilation and the growing armoury of sophisticated weaponry now available were combining to produce a military obsession with overkill and destruction as an end in itself. Goebbels confided to his diary that 'when the first of these missiles screams down onto London, something akin to panic will break out among the British public'.

Certainly there was no defence against the rockets. Launched in Holland, they reached an altitude of sixty miles, moving in a vast parabola at up to 3,600 miles an hour, twice the speed of sound. They took only four minutes before they reached their target, exploding on impact. These space-age missiles – technological marvels of their time – left the British defence system of Spitfires, ack ack and barrage balloons completely redundant. And because the Germans were launching the rockets from trailers that were moved around and camouflaged, the R.A.F. found it impossible to locate and destroy the missiles before they were airborne. People were stunned that Germany could mount another major air offensive against them at a time when government officials had led them to believe that the war had virtually been won. Military setbacks for the Allies in Europe added to the gloom, especially the Arnhem fiasco in late September where there were around 15,000 captured or killed – more than had been lost in the D-day landings – in the abortive attempt to land troops behind the German lines. Had it been successful the action would have resulted in the capture of the rocket launching sites and a more rapid end to the war. Many blamed the government for failing, despite overwhelming Allied strength, to defeat Germany finally, and for leaving London defenceless against the rocket attacks. Government attempts to boost morale by replacing the black-out with a less rigorous 'dim-out' in September, and by ordering the Home Guard to stand down in November, in fact, had the opposite effect. Now that the rockets were raining down on London these measures were thought to be premature. Also the Home Guard had given many thousands of Londoners a pride, a purpose and a real sense of participation in the defence of the capital. Now they felt redundant and powerless to do anything about the new German onslaught. And what was thought to be unnecessary censorship heightened this sense of powerlessness.

By early November many parts of London had been hit, from Bermondsey to Walthamstow and from Camberwell to West Ham, and a public statement was needed to contain the rising tide of anger and anxiety. On 10 November, more than two months after the explosions began, Churchill announced that London was under attack. By this time hundreds of Londoners had been killed, more than a thousand seriously injured, and tens of thousands of houses seriously damaged by the new weapon. News about the rocket attacks had been censored to try to keep people's spirits up, as well as to prevent the German High Command

The aftermath of the worst rocket disaster of the war on 25 November 1944. A missile landed on Woolworth's department store in New Cross, razing it to the ground: 160 were killed and a further 200 injured

from finding out where they had landed. Now the government anxiously watched the effect official news of the rockets would have on Londoners' morale.

The first serious rocket attack that received widespread publicity was the New Cross disaster of 25 November, when a missile scored a direct hit on the Woolworth's department store, packed with Saturday lunchtime shoppers. Bodies were flung skywards and the building crumbled into a tangled mass of bricks and masonry. June Gaida, then thirteen years old, has lasting memories of the appalling aftermath:

> I was going shopping that morning for my mother, and suddenly there was a blinding flash of light, and a roaring, rushing sound. I was thrown into the air. There was noise all around me, a deafening terrible noise that beat against my eardrums and, when I fell to the ground, I curled myself up into a ball to protect myself, and I tried to scream but there wasn't any air. When the noise had faded, I picked myself up and I was coated with brick dust, with slivers of glass in my hair. Then I walked towards Woolworths. Things were still falling out of the sky, there were bricks, masonry, and bits of things and bits of people. I remember seeing a horse's head lying in the gutter. Further on there was a pram-hood all twisted and bent, and there was a little baby's hand still in its woolly sleeve. Outside the pub there was a bus and it had been concertinaed, with rows of people sitting inside, all covered in dust and dead. I looked over towards where Woolworths had been and there was nothing. There was just an enormous gap covered by a cloud of dust and I could see right through to the streets beyond Woolworths. No building, just piles of rubble and bricks, and from underneath it all I could hear people screaming.

The final death toll – although this was not disclosed at the time – was 160, with a further 200 injured, many of them seriously. It was the worst rocket disaster to date and although – as in the reporting of all these incidents – the location, the casualty figures and much of the horrific detail was kept hidden, news of what had happened spread through London. Suddenly Londoners were made painfully aware of the new destructive power of the rockets.

Although knowledge of the rocket attacks did not lead to the panic which some officials feared, it certainly heightened the tension in the capital. For if the flying bombs were seen as sinister, then the rockets brought an element of supernatural terror into the daily lives of Londoners. They were generally more feared because there was no air raid warning and it was impossible to hear them coming or to shelter from them. At least with the doodlebugs Londoners had a sporting chance to escape death in those twelve seconds when people would dive for cover if they heard them cut out above them. Moreover, basements and even Morrisons no longer provided a safe refuge: rockets could penetrate all but the deepest shelters. As a result the rockets made everyone feel vulnerable at all times of the day and night. The feelings of loneliness and isolation aroused during the first weeks of the flying-bomb attacks were reawakened and further aggravated. One man working on war damage repair in the Brixton area saw 'women praying in the street for them to stop the war', something he had never witnessed at the height of the blitz or even of the flying bombs. Mollie Matthews, now a clerk at Tate & Lyle's sugar refinery in Silvertown, was constantly distraught at the death threat the rockets posed to her family while she was away at work:

There were occasions when, if a rocket had dropped locally to where I worked, and I didn't live too far from work, I would go home to see if my mum and sister were O.K. But this particular morning a rocket dropped and I didn't go home because my mum was due to come into work very soon. I received a phone call; the voice was a little incoherent, I couldn't quite understand what was going on, other than the fact that our house had been hit.

I left work, ran out of the gate to catch a bus and no bus came. Every second seemed like ages. Consequently I decided to run home. It was about a three-mile trek so, running and walking and running again, I eventually reached our street. There was ruined houses everywhere; burst pipes, bodies in sacks. When I reached home I found that our house was a skeleton, a mess. I immediately got to the bricks and kept throwing them away, calling out for my mum and my sister and wondering if they were there or not.

Eventually a policeman came and said that some people had been taken to a nearby school. I flew round to the school, but at the gate my legs turned to jelly, and for some reason I just could not move. A gentleman came along and asked what was wrong and I tried to explain to him. He said he would go into the school for me, and they seemed to be the magic words. I thought 'If anyone's got to find them it's got to be me', and with that the use was back in my legs and off I went into the school. I searched through several rooms and eventually there was mum and my sister, covered in dirt and soot where the firemen had

The 'shanty town' streets of Chingford in February 1945 with blasted roof tiles, windows patched with gauze and acres of rubble. London now faced a new housing crisis, with more than a million homes damaged as a result of the doodlebug and rocket attacks

helped them out. Mum was injured, lying on a camp bed, my sister, fortunately, was O.K.

The vast majority of V-2 rockets landed on London's eastern and north-eastern suburbs, or in the old East End. This was completely unintended by the German crews firing the missiles, but resulted from inaccurate aiming, faulty mechanisms and, most important, the fact that all the rockets were fired from Holland and thus passed over Essex and the eastern suburbs on the way to their target of central London. Many were dropping short, as they had during the flying-bomb offensive, but now it was east not south London which took the brunt of the attack. Ilford was the worse-hit area, suffering thirty-five rocket explosions in the last winter of the war, closely followed by West Ham, Barking, Dagenham and Walthamstow. The casualty figures in the north-east corner of the capital were 645 dead and 1441 seriously injured – thirty times as much as the least affected areas in London, like Chelsea, Paddington and Westminster. Heavily built up working-class areas like Islington, Finsbury and Stepney also suffered a higher death rate from the rockets – partly the result of direct hits on tenement buildings.

The effect of the attacks was to fuel class resentment and hostility towards the government, especially in working-class areas. Churchill's private secretary, for example, warned him of a flood of letters from Ilford and the most seriously attacked areas in east London and Essex complaining bitterly about the government's lack of action. The residents of these areas were claiming that a more vigorous attempt would have been made to counter the attack if the main weight had fallen instead on upper-class enclaves like Buckingham Palace or Whitehall. And they demanded immediate military action to end the rocket offensive. This was symptomatic of a growing mood of suspicion and cynicism towards the government. The old idealism and unity of the post-blitz era was increasingly being replaced by a new awareness of class divisions and differences.

But the main cause of this growing class antagonism in the capital during the last winter of the war went deeper than the social geography of the rocket 'hits'. The onslaught of missiles aggravated and heightened a number of major social problems and conflicts that had created discontent in the capital for some time. Inadequate housing was foremost amongst these problems and it again became a major issue at this time.

Even before the blitz took its toll on London's housing stock back in the early stages of the war, there had been severe overcrowding in the capital and many thousands of dwellings were considered barely fit for habitation. Although efforts were made to patch up damaged houses after the blitz, the repairs were totally inadequate because most of the labour force had been channelled into the war production drive. On top of all this the flying-bomb attacks had damaged more than a million and a quarter houses in London – almost half of the capital's housing stock. By the last months of the war something approaching 130,000 houses had been destroyed or damaged beyond repair. Mass evacuation and the temporary patching up of 750,000 houses had postponed an immediate crisis. But the devastating effect of the V-2 aerial attack on London's housing, together with the return of many evacuees, combined to produce a desperate shortage of accommodation during the winter of 1944-5. The rocket attacks flattened thousands of houses and shattered millions of window panes as they exploded onto the capital. Some districts were by now beginning to look like shanty towns. Those worst affected were London's working-class areas because their housing was often of poor quality and high density and as such most vulnerable to bomb damage. Also, the residents of those districts were less likely to have the money to command

An emergency repair squad fixes tarpaulin to the roof of a suburban 'semi' wrecked by rocket blast. An average of 1,500 homes were damaged every time a doodlebug or rocket landed

rapid private repairs. Ironically, although Charlie Draper repaired houses for a living, he and his family in Peckham were also victims of this housing crisis:

> We waited a hell of a time for repairs to be done to the house. The roof got blown off, windows caved in and we were waiting for repairs to be done. We couldn't just get the materials and do it ourselves because there was none available. So we had to wait for the council to come round and do them, which took a long time. We only had temporary repairs, a tarpaulin on the roof just to keep the water out. The water eventually did creep in down the sides, and most people moved from the top of their houses downstairs into the bottom to keep dry.

The situation was at its worst in January 1945. During this month V-2 rockets landed on London at the increased rate of five every day. This coincided with the coldest winter weather in living memory. Many householders – especially working-class families – were already living in primitive conditions with broken roofs, blown-out and papered-over windows, missing doors, smashed pipes and an irregular gas, electricity and coal supply. Now the Arctic winds, snow and sleet made the conditions practically intolerable. Many went down with frostbite, hypothermia, rheumatism, and there was a flu' epidemic. Appalling housing conditions aggravated Charlie Drapers's bad health:

> I was taken with rheumatic fever. I was paralysed for four weeks and the time I was lying in bed, there was no roof, there was just the tarpaulin, the canvas up over the windows and half the fireplace missing. I just lay there waiting for the repairs to be done. And there was a sort of damp atmosphere that didn't do the rheumatic fever any good, because there was no way we could keep the house warm in those conditions. It laid me up for six weeks altogether.

Absenteeism again became a major problem at work and tens of thousands of hours were lost in factories and offices because of illness. Londoners were weak, exhausted, and longed for the end of the war. Mollie Matthews recalls:

> I think there came a time when it must have affected everybody the same way. We were tired, the war had been on for six years, we had suffered from it and the rockets. And this last incident, with the rocket destroying our house had its effect, because eventually I began to feel quite tired. Obviously it was showing at work. One thing, I wanted to wear nothing but dark clothes because I thought they stayed cleaner longer, they wouldn't show the dirt. Eventually the firm for which I worked sent me away to a convalescent home at Tadworth in Surrey for a little while.

But at the same time people increasingly worried about what would happen in the future. By now so much damage had been done to London's housing stock that earlier hopes of a brave new world after the war seemed to be becoming pipe dreams. The older generation, in addition, remembered the broken promise of 'homes for heroes' after the First World War. It all contributed to a mood of anger, suspicion, cynicism and sometimes despair. Public opinion surveys of the time all reported a great concern with the housing crisis in the capital coupled with a lack of faith by the less well-off in the capacity of any post-war government to solve the problem.

Another important cause for concern amongst working-class people was unemployment. There was widespread fear that the winding-up of war production when victory was won would result in a considerable increase in unemployment, as had happened after the First World War. This concern was particularly great among women, who expected to be made redundant when the war ended and the troops returned from the front: indeed, this was often written into their contracts. The response of many workers was to try to secure their position or to get as much as they could while they were assured of a job.

Whereas in the crisis period of 1940-41 there were virtually no strikes, the last year of the war produced a wave of stoppages and disputes in the capital. There were serious strikes in the docks, amongst London Transport workers and in the new engineering factories in the north-western industrial belt. What makes this unrest all the more significant was that strikes had been declared illegal by the government since the beginning of the war, strikers could be and were fined and imprisoned, and the press was extremely hostile to anyone taking such action.

Also underlying the resurgence of disputes was a new conflict between management and workers over industrial relationships in the post-war world. Both sides had made sacrifices during the great production drive to win the war but now that the war seemed to be virtually over, they both looked more and more to winning for themselves the best possible deal for the future. Management sought to end war-time concessions and privileges for workers, while the workers themselves took advantage of their strong bargaining position to try to institutionalize war-time gains. It seemed that the spirit of national unity and idealism generated by the war was fading. Charlie Draper's experience in the housing repair business reflected the change in mood:

> We'd put up with the guvnor and he'd put up with us because we had no choice. We had to by law, we couldn't leave and everyone was doing their bit, but by the end of the war there was a lot of bad feeling creeping in. My guvnor was keeping back all my £1 10s a week over-time I earned; he kept saying the cheque hadn't come through from the Ministry. I found out later he was doing this with everybody and salting it away for the future after the war. And he was fiddling our time and work sheets that he sent to the Ministry. He said we were doing more repair work than we were, and he gave us an extra quid a week to keep our mouths shut. I ended up leaving; the trust had broken down.

Although many Londoners looked forward to the post-war world with

During the last winter of the war many families were living in primitive conditions with blown-out windows, missing doors and an irregular gas and water supply. This coincided with the worst weather in living memory: many people fell victim to frost bite, hypothermia and flu

great apprehension, by early 1945 there was a desperate desire for the war to end immediately. This was not defeatism: the vast majority were determined to see it through to the bitter end no matter what sacrifices they had to make. But Londoners were tired of the deprivations of bomb-blasted housing, rationing and the ever-present threat of death. A deep frustration with the way the war was dragging on was swelling up.

Increasingly people blamed the Germans who, it was felt, were refusing to accept the inevitable, their defeat. An intense anti-German feeling gripped the capital at this time. While Londoners had seldom had any doubts that Nazism was evil, many had been able to dissociate this from the ordinary German civilian, who was seen, to some extent, to be trapped by the fascist state. By this stage of the war, however, people extended their hatred of the repressive fascist system they were fighting against to a hatred of all Germans as a people. This was primarily caused by the endless and seemingly pointless attacks on the capital, though it was also fuelled by revelations about the true horrors of the Nazi regime and its concentration camps that were by now beginning to filter through. The end result was a new mood, encouraged by the newsreels and the press, that wanted revenge and retribution against the German people. There was a widespread feeling that Germany should be bombed into submission whatever the consequences. Len Jones, whose military designs were one factor that made the bombing of German cities more accurate, remembers this new climate of opinion:

> You hated Germany, you hated Germans, a bad thing, a horrible feeling, really. I only recognize it as sadistic now, but you must understand it was a desensitizing of moral values. Because there was this overwhelming feeling on everybody's part who was involved, it was revenge. Part of me hated the idea of German cities being damaged, because they were beautiful places, I loved German architecture, but at that stage you felt your whole character was changing and you wanted to punish them. You wondered where all this madness was going to end.

The Allied bombing of Dresden, ordered by Churchill, on 13 February 1945, came as the climax of this new mood. The city was almost completely destroyed, consumed by a fire-storm and an unknown number of citizens perished – perhaps as many as 100,000, around three times the number of London civilians killed during the entire war. It was a merciless action which many people have argued had little, if any, military significance.

In retaliation the Germans fired rocket after rocket towards the heart of London; attacks which, in turn, had no strategic significance whatsoever for Germany now faced certain defeat. Until almost the end of March London continued to suffer casualties from rocket attacks, though the scale of death was small by comparison to Dresden, with tens rather than thousands of people being killed. Nevertheless the attacks seemed to be wanton acts of violence.

But although this increasingly hard attitude to civilian killings was yet to reach its climax on the international front, for London at least the horrors were soon to be over. On 29 March all rocket units were withdrawn from Holland into Germany. There were to be no more air raids on London or anywhere else in Britain. Victory over Germany was now only weeks away.

6
A NEW LIFE

As Big Ben struck three o'clock on the afternoon of 8 May 1945, silence descended on the vast crowd which had gathered in Whitehall to celebrate Victory in Europe. Over the loudspeakers, specially erected for the occasion, came the voice of the Prime Minister, Winston Churchill. His was the only voice to be heard. The crowd of thousands hung on every word. As Churchill announced the end of hostilities with Germany, they all cheered loudly. This was followed by cries of joy and a waving of hats and flags as he declared that 'The German war is, therefore, at an end'.

It had been clear for weeks that Germany had been beaten by the Allies and ever since Hitler had committed suicide at the end of April, the final collapse of the Third Reich had been imminent. Indeed, the announcement of the Nazi Supreme Command's unconditional surrender had come the day before. Nevertheless the official announcement of peace in Europe on VE day itself sparked off deep feelings of patriotic pride and relief as Londoners released the tensions and pressures of the past six years.

London, having taken the brunt of the German air attack, had earned its place at the centre of the celebrations. That evening the crowds in the focal points of the capital went wild. In Trafalgar Square, lines of young women and servicemen linked arms and swung along the road singing 'Roll out the barrel', 'Two lovely black eyes', 'Oh, you great big beautiful doll' and many other songs. Women swiftly lost count of the number of men they'd kissed. In Leicester Square, people hung together all trying to do the Conga. In Piccadilly Circus, a sailor stripped off his clothes and climbed on to the top of the Eros pedestal, wrapping a Union Jack around himself. As midnight approached the excitement became more infectious and the crowds more boisterous. Amongst them was Charlie Draper:

Previous pages: Late night revellers in the West End celebrate VJ day, the official end of the war, 15 August 1945. The feeling that day was primarily one of relief: at last the suffering, the destruction and the pain of war was over

VE day, 8 May 1945. Inset: Dancing in the streets in Walthamstow, as the residents of Bedford Road celebrate with a victory tea. Note the absence of men who were not yet demobbed from the services or released from war work. Right: Mothers and children enjoy a well-earned VE day feast outside The Ship in Long Lane, Borough

Everybody was just going mad and dancing and singing in the streets. Me and my mates had a few drinks and I ended up in the pool in Trafalgar Square. I think it was one of those occasions when I thought, 'Well, they didn't get me', and I was lucky to survive it and I thought, 'Well, that's it, I'll have a good drink and celebrate the fact that I'm still alive.' I must have ended up in St James's Park that night, sleeping there, because that's where I found myself the next morning.

In the suburbs the celebrations were more subdued, though the sense of excitement was still present. Most houses were decorated with bunting, Union Jacks or fairy lights. There were street parties, fireworks and bonfires. In some places, an effigy of Hitler had the pride of place on the fire: the surrounding crowds would cheer as it was consumed by flames. As the evening wore on, pianos were sometimes carried into the streets and there would be sing-alongs and dancing to the old Cockney favourites like 'The Lambeth Walk' or 'Knees up Mother Brown'.

But on the following day, when the immediate excitement had passed, there was a feeling of anti-climax. Though the European war had ended, the world war went on. In the Far East the Allies were still at battle with the Japanese. British troops were still dying. In London, however, people could now wind down from their long, hard struggle. But as they did the sense of purpose generated by the war was replaced by a vacuum. People were very unsure about what the future would bring. During the war London had changed in all sorts of ways and Londoners themselves had, despite the hardships, experienced new opportunities. As a result people had changed expectations both for themselves and for the kind of city they thought London could be. What was to come out of all these changes? What would be the legacy of the war on London and on the life of Londoners?

Perhaps most important the war had taken a large number of Londoners away from where they had been born and brought up. Evacuation had affected enormous numbers of Londoners. During the course of the war some 2 million people had been moved at least for a short time away from London, and probably 500,000 had stayed away for more than a year. The cumulative effect of these successive waves of evacuation was to change many Londoners' perceptions of what 'home' was like. Though at the outset, evacuation had been most unsuccessful, during the later stages of the war many of the problems had been ironed out. Many of the evacuees began to appreciate their new settings. They had often come from London's poorest communities and up till then had known only damp and crowded tenement blocks, verminous back-to-backs and dirty streets. Now they had come to know open air, the countryside and houses that were often in substantially better physical condition. Some of the younger children had been away so long that they had only faded memories of their London homes; for them home was now a village or a small provincial town. Many mothers had been evacuated with the younger children and now had expectations of a house with more room – a separate kitchen and dining room, a bath – and a little garden for the children to play in.

They hoped to live somewhere near a park or the countryside so that their children could continue to have the benefits of fresh air and exercise. The horizons of Londoners had broadened. Being evacuated in Caversham had a profound effect on Gladys Strelitz and her family's ideas about where they were going to live when the war was over:

> It changed my mind decidedly because it was so beautiful there, all the different trees, especially in the springtime and the autumn. The children were so happy, and they could run and have a dip, and Mother always had the towel ready to wipe their feet. We decided that we couldn't go back and live in East Ham any longer, we'd got to get out of London, let the children see the beauty of the countryside, go where there were nice surroundings. We went first to Ilford and then we ended up in Romford. The children used to collect walnuts and there'd be apple trees there they could shake.

Although Doreen Holloway was to begin with very unhappy in her billet in the village of Binfield, Berkshire, she came to develop a love of the countryside which later influenced her to move out from Battersea to Wimbledon:

> We used to walk the lanes as far as White Waltham and Ascot. In fact, almost every day we went out on these nature walks with our teacher and I came to appreciate the lovely countryside, the trees and hedgerows, which were quite in contrast to Battersea, where I came from. I'd never seen primroses and bluebells and that sort of thing before. I hoped that when the war was over, should I ever marry, I would certainly like a garden of my own. I remembered all this lovely beauty that I had seen.

Many other Londoners also moved out of the capital during the war. Young men, instead of going into the traditional jobs their fathers had done in their local neighbourhood, found a whole new world opened up to them. Military service, in particular, took them away from their locality to exotic locations in Italy and the Middle East, or to postings in other parts of Britain. Some met up with local girls, or personnel in their station, and married. Their attachments to their own London communities waned.

Young women, too, often found that military service gave them the opportunity to get away from the limited options that their local communities held out for them. For example, young girls who would have got married and had children in the area in which they were brought up, joined the Auxiliary Territorial Service (A.T.S.), the Women's Royal Naval Service (W.R.N.S.) or the Women's Auxiliary Air Force (W.A.A.F.) and travelled to distant parts, meeting a wide cross-section of people. In addition, many London girls opted for the Land Army with its outdoor life on the farms. Others were directed to factory work, often in the Midlands, where they stayed in hostels. The expectations of these young women changed completely. Nina Hibbin remembers:

Before the war, there was virtually no way well-brought-up young women could leave home, and the prospect was simply that you got married to leave home. And now suddenly there was this possibility of joining the W.A.A.F. People did feel very strongly about doing their bit for the war, but the W.A.A.F. or any of the services had this attraction because we knew that we would learn a trade, we would travel, and that's what people wanted to do. It was a great tragedy if anybody joined the W.A.A.F. and was posted back home. So I think because women's aspirations were so much less developed that they are now, just the mere fact of leaving home meant a lot, being free from the chores that were expected of women, for, you know, women were expected to be domesticated. So, there was a lot of freedom in this life-style. Of course there was a lot of sexual freedom, because all of a sudden there we were, men and women altogether, in a way that would have been impossible before. Mums would have been on our backs if we'd been at home. We were often posted from one place to the other, meeting different people, from different countries even, so that our lives were broadened out quite a bit. A lot of us used to say, 'We'll never go back to the kind of people that we were before the war.' We had learned trades, or had travelled a bit over the country, so we got this feeling of being somebody, rather than just a very domesticated person. I think we wanted more when we got back home. I certainly did.

Evacuated London mothers and their children enjoy fresh air and beautiful countryside in Grasmere, in the Lake District. During the war around two million Londoners had moved away from the capital, the long-term effect of which was to broaden their horizons and loosen their attachments to their old communities

Other Londoners who never actually left the capital nevertheless moved around within it. Unmarried women who did not enter the services were directed to work in war production and this often meant moving away from home, to live in places like Acton and Slough. For even more women it meant leaving a life of domestic service in the grand houses of Belgravia, Kensington and Hampstead. These new jobs offered greater freedom and independence and many were not prepared to go back to a narrow and restricted life in service after the war. As a result, servant-keeping amongst wealthy London households declined as maids, cooks and tweenies looked for a new life in factories and offices.

Those men who were exempt from military service because they worked in essential industries often found that their work also took them away to different parts of the capital. Many who were born and bred in inner areas like Bermondsey, Poplar and Islington went to the outer suburbs, in particular the industrial belts of the north-west, north-east and south of London. By the end of the war they had often settled in the areas where they now worked. Len Jones was one of the many thousands who moved out from the East End, 'A few months after coming to Carshalton we rented a little house, and then as the war went on, I was earning very good money, so in 1944 I bought the little house across the road. The work was here, so we stayed out here. This was now our home, Carshalton'.

The bombing too had a tremendous impact on shifting people away from their homes. During the course of the war, destruction resulting either from conventional bombing or the new V-weapons had made at least 1,500,000 Londoners homeless, some for a short period of time others for months or years. As with the evacuees, the homeless were most likely to come from the inner London boroughs. During the blitz, in particular, many homeless families in the old East End and in declining inner areas like Battersea and Hackney had been unable to find accommodation in their neighbourhood and had moved in with relations or friends in distant parts of the capital. As the war progressed, they often found accommodation of their own in that area. Others had been officially billeted in more prosperous parts of London, like Edgware and Finchley. Billeting, again like evacuation, had at first caused problems, but eventually many families came to prefer the less crowded environments in which they were 'temporarily' living. Emily Golder recalls:

> After we'd stopped in Finchley for a while, I looked around and realized what a lovely place it was to live in. All the greenery, so different from the back-to-backs in the docks area, with outside toilets, smut, smoke and everything. This is where I decided I wanted to fetch children up when I eventually got married. There was no comparison with the East End; this was a residential area. So I had my son in Finchley and he went to the school down the road. It was very good, we were very happy. The houses had lovely gardens, so different to the East End with just the backyard. So we settled down in Finchley.

Whatever the causes, these upheavals of London's population were by far the greatest and most concentrated shifts the capital had ever seen. Out of a total of 8,000,000 people, at least a third to a half had moved away from their neighbourhood for some period of the war. This enormous movement of people was particularly sharp in inner London and, moreover, permanent. For a long time numbers in London's poorest boroughs had been declining, but the impact of the war years was devastating; Stepney's population, for example, had dropped during the 1930s by about two per cent a year; during the six years of the war it dropped by over forty per cent. While some yearned to move back, for many the ties had been broken.

But even those Londoners who had stayed within their local community throughout the war often found that their expectations and aspirations had been changed by the social upheavals of these years in such a way that they no longer identified so closely with their communities. Young women, in particular, often made a far wider range of friends. With fathers, fiancés and husbands posted away from home they had the opportunity to go out on their own to the dance halls. This sort of independence would have been widely regarded as immoral in the pre-war years. There they could meet servicemen not just from all over Britain but also from many of the Allied countries. The American G.I.s, in particular, offered the chance of easy friendship, uninhibited by the conventions of class and respectability by which many Londoners had been brought up. Some of these friendships led to marriage and a permanent uprooting of women from their London homes. More often the friendships would be casual, giving rise to grave concern among the older generation about a decline in moral standards. But for the young women themselves the chance to meet people from very different backgrounds changed their expectations. For example, the G.I.s, unfettered by convention would unashamedly walk into hotels like the Savoy or the Ritz, hitherto preserves of the upper classes. Their philosophy was that if you had the money – and they did – then old-fashioned class barriers should not stand in the way. For the young London women accompanying them, their horizons of what was possible were broadened, as Odette Lesley remembers:

> You see, coming to the Hammersmith Palais made a vast difference to us. We started to meet G.I.s, Canadians, boys from other countries, and we used to sit and talk to them, and listen to their stories of where they came from, exotic names like Texas, New York, Montreal, names we'd only seen and heard in films. And when we listened to their way of life, we realized that there was a very big new world out there, that we knew nothing about at all. All I knew, for instance, was my little bit of north London, where I'd been brought up; the local streets, my neighbours, and the local dance hall. But I was hearing these marvellous stories, and they opened up horizons to such an extent that I thought I might even see those places one day, I might go there. And I felt a strong sense of independence as a girl that I'd never felt before. It was so exciting, I felt anything was possible.

At the same time new independence sometimes meant that, come the end of the war, women who were recently married were far from sure that they wanted to settle back down with their husbands. Perhaps under the pressures of war, they had married hastily; often their husbands had been away for years, coming home at most for a few week's leave. Divorce, which in the pre-war years had been rare, was set to become much more common. Apart from the sometimes traumatic effects on the individuals

Oil and grease fitters about to take their lunch break at the British Restaurant in Woolmore Street, Poplar, 1943. War work for women encouraged a new independence and many were unprepared to go back to a life in service after the war

involved, for London this again disrupted the settled pre-war patterns of community life. Odette Lesley ended up living in the Channel Islands for a time after escaping from her marriage:

> Like a lot of girls, I really married in quite a hurry in war time. The men were in the services. We knew they were going away, going abroad, and we felt we wanted to get married. I was married when I was eighteen, and I got married on the Tuesday, and Wednesday I was saying goodbye to him. I saw him very briefly after that, and then it was three years before I saw him again. And, of course, because I had changed through the war, through the experiences, meeting all sorts of people, I'd got this sense of independence, which coloured everything I thought about. Then I started to think about my husband. I had awful guilty feelings because I was sure that there was no way when he came home that I'd be able to settle down, into the rather dull, domestic routine which was what he would have expected. I thought to myself, 'I can't stay with him, because I can't do what he wants, I want more out of life now, I want to have more experiences.' In fact, when he was sent back to his unit for demob', I ran off to the Channel Islands, because I knew I couldn't cope with that sort of marriage and that was the end of it. This, of course, was the effect of war.

All these social changes meant that by 1945 many Londoners no longer wanted to live in the communities in which they had lived throughout the pre-war years. In particular, many who had lived in inner London had expectations of a life beyond the back-to-backs and tenements of their youth. At the same time, many Londoners could not return to the streets they had known, even if they wanted, for those streets were often no longer there. Len Jones recalls:

> In some ways I would have loved to have come back to the East End at the end of the war, but where I used to live in Poplar was all blown to

pieces. You see, I missed the wonderful community in the East End and the social life, going down the People's Palace every Friday and Saturday night with my friends. Carshalton was dead in comparison, there was nothing to do. It made me depressed being there, but I decided to stay because I worked in the area and there was really nowhere else to go.

While overall London did not suffer anything like the devastation of many German cities, and in particular Berlin, parts of inner and eastern London were severely hit. In Stepney, forty per cent of the housing was destroyed or badly damaged; in Bermondsey some twenty-five per cent of the dwellings and half the schools and public buildings had been destroyed or demolished. And in Walthamstow, hit heavily by the rockets, over twenty per cent of the houses were totally destroyed or heavily damaged.

During the war, there had been much discussion of how these communities could not just be rebuilt but developed into a new and better form. There had been a surge of interest in reconstruction, which had its seeds in the blitz. For while the Londoners whose homes had been destroyed reflected with pain and grief on their loss, planners and the middle-class reformers began to see the destruction as opening up new opportunities. Hitler had swept away more slums in a few months than radical campaigners had in years or even decades. A new London could rise like a phoenix out of the ashes. The unplanned, chaotic development of London over the centuries could be replaced by a planned London. The poet Louis MacNeice, for example, wrote in *Picture Post* that, as he watched buildings burn during the great raids in May 1941: 'There was a voice inside me which (ignoring all the suffering and wastage involved) kept saying: "Let her go up!" or "Let her come down. Let them all go. Write them all off. Stone walls do not a city make. Tear all the blotted pages out of the book".'

Front cover of a booklet published in October 1942 containing the Royal Academy's vision of a new London. One feature was a monumental stairway leading from the banks of the River Thames to the steps of St Paul's Cathedral

It was a planner's dream. During the rest of the war, plans for the reconstruction of London, and in particular the central areas, abounded. Some were futuristic while others yearned for a recapturing of an older, Renaissance style. Both camps were, in their different ways, idealistic: they envisaged a rejuvenated city, with more open spaces for people to walk through, and wide vistas leading up to the great buildings of London's heritage.

The Royal Academy, representing the more traditional school, published in October 1942 'London Replanned', a thirty-page outline of ambitious projects for the central area. At its heart was the reconstruction of the rubble around St Paul's Cathedral. They envisaged a monumental stairway leading from the banks of the Thames to the steps of St Paul's, with classical pavillions on either side and a new approach to the cathedral from the west consisting of an avenue of trees along a widened Ludgate Hill, opening up into a circular piazza reminiscent of St Peter's, Rome. Another wide vista was to be created between New Oxford Street and the British Museum, by sweeping away the intervening buildings. In Covent Garden, the Academy suggested – somewhat prophetically – that the fruit and vegetable market be replaced by a new music and drama centre and garden, carefully preserving the old colonnades of the market. South of the river, they proposed a new circular park, slightly bigger than Regents's Park, at St George's Circus, Southwark.

In contrasting styles, other architects also put forward a range of plans for opening up new vistas in central London. Two private architects, Kenneth Lindy and Winton Lewis, for example, proposed new focal points such as a five-hundred-foot tower modelled on New York's famous Woolworth's building; they also, more futuristically, proposed a giant helicopter landing pad stretching into the sky above Liverpool Street Station.

Many of these schemes were little more than the daydreams of architects and planners and had little chance of ever getting off the ground. Much more influential, however, were two major studies, the County of London Plan and the Greater London Plan, commissioned by the London County Council and headed by Sir Patrick Abercrombie, Professor of Town Planning at London University. These were comprehensive plans for the rebuilding of London covering all aspects of the city's life. By far the most important subject to be tackled was housing.

Just as the 1942 Beveridge Report with its plan to eliminate the social evils of want, squalor, illness, ignorance and disease, by building a welfare state, had captured people's desire for a post-war world free of poverty, so too the Abercrombie plans reflected an ambition for a slum-free London. There was to be a radical reconstruction of the Victorian heart of the capital. Those mean streets which had not been destroyed by the Luftwaffe would be swept away by the planners to enable new and planned communities to be built. In each 'neighbourhood', which would house about 10,000 people, there would be a central area with open space and community facilities such as a school, nursery, health centre and shops. Historic features, such as churches, would be preserved to form focal points. Around these would be a mix of modern terraced houses with small gardens and high-rise flats. With the advantage of hindsight,

The blitz was a planner's dream and in its aftermath many schemes for redevelopment were drawn up. Above: *A vision of a modern, planned community in the capital after the war. With the advantage of hindsight, parts of the plan, especially the enthusiasm for tower blocks, look less than ideal, but at the time it was seen as holding out the prospect of a new life for Londoners.* Left: *Lindy and Lewis's 1944 plan for a 500-foot skyrise office block behind the Guildhall, modelled on the Woolworth's building in New York*

these plans – and in particular the ill-fated tower blocks – look less than ideal. But they were seen at the time as holding out the prospect of a new and better life for everyone.

This noble aim was seen to be overwhelmingly important. The war had brought out a strong belief that the 'ordinary' Londoner deserved a better deal. The people of London had been the heroes of the day and had been celebrated as such. And hand in hand with the realization that winning the war depended to an unprecedented degree on the effort and determination of the civilian population, went a greater readiness to respond to people's needs and wishes.

Entertainment, for example, became much more orientated towards a mass audience. The B.B.C., which in the pre-war years had been elitist, offering its listeners a diet of high culture, began to introduced a wide range of popular programmes. Dance halls which had previously imposed a rather staid style, some banning songs such as 'Knees up Mother Brown', gave way to popular demands. Managements had, for example, tried to ban the jitter-bug when it arrived with the first American G.I.s in 1942. The dance's exuberant style and violent gymnastics, sometimes ending up with the female partner being swung around with her feet off the floor, were hardly in keeping with the 'respectable', traditional image the dance halls had tried to cultivate. But the demand for the jitter-bug spread like wildfire and it wasn't long before the managements of London's dance halls were forced to take down their 'no jitter-bugging' notices.

People's views on the fairness of traditional structures of society were also changing. Given that the 'ordinary' Londoner was contributing so much to the war effort, people began to question the privileges of the wealthy minority. For example, Jerome Willis, a reporter for the London *Evening Standard*, wrote of the blitz: 'I wondered then if those citizens who stayed to work in the stricken capital would have much of a voice in the promised post-war economic changes, or would those who owned most of it, but had stayed very far away from it when the bombs were falling, come back again to reign?'

'Oversexed, overpaid and over here': G.I.s jitter-bugging with London women in 1944. The Americans helped to break down old-fashioned conventions and class barriers in the capital

The war was opening the eyes of the middle classes to poverty in their midst. Through billeting, comfortably well-off households in the suburbs were brought face to face with hardship which in the pre-war years had gone ignored. At first, the shock of the squalor, the filth and the bad manners had sometimes produced an unsympathetic reaction but gradually, as the better-off households got to know and like the poorer families billeted on them, they began to see the problem of poverty not in terms of the failings of the poor but in terms of the unfairness of society. At the

same time, many middle-class women had joined the W.V.S. and their
voluntary work during the blitz, helping families who had been bombed
out, had again made the privileged more aware of the conditions in which
London's poor lived. There was, in particular, a substantial shift of opinion among the middle classes in favour of greater welfare provision by the
state. Vera Michel-Downes, active throughout the war in voluntary work
in the capital, remembers the new moral climate:

> A wonderful spirit of caring developed during the war. People had
> been thrown together in rest centres and shelters, and they really got to
> know each other and helped each other. There was a tremendous
> amount of voluntary social work of one sort or another going on, espe-
> cially in the W.V.S., and it heightened people's awareness of social
> problems and poverty. Snobbery and class differences became far less
> important, people just wanted to help each other.

Hand in hand with this growing support for 'welfarism' came a growing desire for a more equal society. This stemmed, at least in part, from a
much greater social mixing during the war. Pre-war London had
remained sharply divided by class but in war-time London people from
all sorts of backgrounds had met in civil defence, in the Home Guard, at
work, at leisure. Close friendships were often formed between people
whose backgrounds were so different that before the war they would
have had little chance of meeting socially. Londoners hoped that in the
post-war world people would be judged on their own merits and not on
their background. It was a desire for a kind of classless London.

By 1941, the Home Intelligence reports on London were recording
widespread support for 'home-grown socialism' which was 'growing like
a jungle plant'. Londoners believed that everyone was entitled to decent
housing, good health, equal opportunities and an adequate standard of
living and, moreover, that the state had a responsibility to ensure that
every citizen gained these rights. These aspirations were to some extent
reflected and reinforced in government propaganda. The Ministry of
Information and the Army Bureau of Current Affairs appreciated that visions of a better future were an important motivation to help people pull
through the war. Though Churchill consistently opposed making promises of social reform, many radical ideas did seep through in government
propaganda. The result was that both the M.O.I. and A.B.C.A. produced
an influential series of propaganda posters and films heralding a better,
fairer society after the war, a society really worth fighting for. One
A.B.C.A. poster, for example, pictured the new Finsbury health centre
emerging from the disease and poverty of the past. Government propaganda films like 'Post 23' talked of the new spirit of unity leading to a better world for all, while others like 'Five and Under' praised the growth of
welfare services.

Towards the end of the war, many Londoners had begun to fear that
these aspirations would turn out to be nothing but a dream. Many of the
opportunities created by the war began to close up. This was particularly
true for women, who often found themselves thrown out of their jobs

when men returned from the services. Admittedly many of the women were tired from the pressures of full-time work on top of the burden of running a household single-handed under the conditions of war-time rationing, most had appreciated the new independence that paid work gave them, the satisfaction of doing a skilled manual job, and the companionship of their workmates. Many wanted to carry on working in their new jobs but as the war came to its close the sexual inequalities of the pre-war years began to be reasserted. Nina Hibbin, having established herself as a flight mechanic at Hendon, found there was no future for her in this job:

> At the end of the war, what I wanted to do was to be a mechanic. I went to my Warrant Officer, who thought a lot of me as a flight mechanic, knew I could do the job, and I said, 'What are the chances of me getting on a course?' But he just laughed and said, 'Forget it, duck', you know the way they do. I tried. I mean, I wrote to lots of firms, I went to lots of garages, but it was absolutely inconceivable at that time. After I'd tried everywhere I did what I suppose was the next best thing, I trained to become a teacher.
>
> I went on an emergency training course and, although teaching is a very fine profession, it was second best, it was a sort of compromise as far as I was concerned. And I think that's what probably happened to a lot of women, their horizons were opened out, and they wanted to do all kinds of things, but then even before the war was over, the pressures began to come down. Now the boys are coming back, you must go home and you must get ready to make homes and so forth. And I think that the best any of us could do was a compromise of some sort.

'Your Britain: Fight For It Now.' A propaganda poster produced in 1943 by A.B.C.A. – The Army Bureau Of Current Affairs – encouraging people to believe they were fighting for a better Britain in which poverty and disease would be swept away

At the same time, some of the unity of earlier years began to disappear. People were slipping back into the habits of pre-war years. For example, in the House of Commons factory where, during the war years, every worker, whether they were a duke or a doorman, had been on equal terms, the atmosphere of classlessness rapidly evaporated. Vera Michel-Downes was the welfare officer at the factory:

When we were closed down, although we ended up with a wonderful party and everybody had a fantastic time, the moment the factory was closed all the class barriers raised their ugly heads again. Immediately we were back to surnames and deferential attitudes towards people. Although everybody was congratulating everybody on a wonderful job done, it was quite interesting to see that the barriers remained there and were reinstated the moment the war was over.

But soon after VE day, Londoners were given the chance to reassert their desire for a new and more equal post-war London. On 23 May, the coalition government, which had been in power for the past five years, came to an end at the insistence of the Labour members. Churchill tendered his resignation as Prime Minister and a general election campaign got underway.

Despite the evidence of strong support for socialist ideals, it was generally expected that Churchill's leadership of the Conservative Party would prove decisive. He had led Britain to victory and confidently expected to lead the nation into peace. But when the result was announced on 26 July, the political upturn of the century had taken place. Labour, led by the mild and studious Clem Attlee, won a landslide victory. Churchill was identified with the past, the Labour Party with the future. While Churchill had held out against social reform during the war, the Labour Party had always been identified with more and better welfare. While Churchill emphasized the importance of pursuing the war against Japan to its end, Labour talked of new housing and an end to the slums.

The mood in London was clear. Across the capital, there was an eighteen per cent swing from the Conservatives to Labour, one of the highest in the country. Labour had more votes than the Conservatives in every district in London except the business areas of the centre. The suburbs, once upon a time Tory strongholds, turned to Labour as the middle classes voted for change. In Lewisham, Herbert Morrison, the Minister for Home Security during the war, turned a safe Conservative majority into a Labour majority of 15,000.

In inner London, the vote for radicalism was overwhelming. In Fulham, Islington, St Pancras and Hammersmith, the left-wing parties of Labour, Common Wealth and Communist parties polled sixty-five per cent of the vote compared to thirty-four per cent for the Tories, a sharp reversal of the position in the last general election in 1935, when the Tories had a majority over the left of fifty-two per cent to forty-six per cent. In the traditional Labour strongholds to the east of the City, the Tories were decimated: in the boroughs of Stoke Newington, Hackney, Shoreditch and Finsbury, the left polled over seventy-two per cent of the

Clem Attlee and the London Labour Party celebrate their dramatic election victory, the political upturn of the century

vote. The mood of radicalism in the inner eastern areas was such that in the seats in which the Communist Party stood, they succeeded in replacing the Conservatives for second place, polling thirty-three per cent of the vote. And London's first-ever Communist Member of Parliament was elected with the success of Phil Piratin in Mile End.

Londoners' hopes were high. Nina Hibbin remembers the atmosphere at Hendon Aerodrome as the election results came in:

> There was a hut that was used for lectures and we had a huge map of the whole of the country there, with all the constituencies marked. As the results came through on the radio, we were sticking in red pins for the Labour victories, and blue ones for the Tory victories, and there was a huge crowd outside that gathered all day. There were great cheers every time there was another Labour victory, because we really did feel that this was socialism, that things are going to change, it was going to be our country after all. There was a great 'us and them' feeling and it was going to be 'us' at last, particularly, let's say, to do with housing. Because a lot of people thought that the blitz, however tragic it was, was doing the job that ought to have been done a long time ago, which was the removal of the slums. We'd seen the exhibitions for a new London and we imagined that there would be splendid housing estates, gardens, and facilities for everyone. And so we thought, right, there's this marvellous victory, the whole country is wanting a new kind of Britain that would work for us, and not for them. And this was the vision, and as each pin went into the map great cheers went up, we really thought that was it.

Charlie Draper, who had recently joined the Labour Party League of Youth, believed a new and better London might now be built:

Well, when I saw a Labour government being elected I thought, 'This is great.' I thought that they would make London a better place, because where I used to live it was slum conditions, people living on top of one another. I wanted to see something different, new estates, new playing fields for the children, better living conditions, better environment where there was more spaces. A nice new London.

But the problems, especially in the inner areas, were huge. In addition, as the war drew to its close, Britain faced a new crisis: a financial Dunkirk. The costs of the war had been enormous and Britain had depended heavily on loans from the United States. When the world war finally came to an end on 14 August, following Japan's surrender after the bombing of Hiroshima and Nagasaki, the United States ended these lend-lease agreements.

The plans for the rebuilding of inner London began to seem somewhat more distant. But for the people who had been displaced from their homes during the war and who had gained new expectations for life after the war, it was, now, the present they looked to for this better life and not the future. If the inner areas in which they had been born and brought up could not offer the rejuvenated life held out during the war in the ambitious plans for London, then these inner Londoners would have to look elsewhere. And they did. They moved out to the suburbs and the new towns around London, sometimes with a touch of sadness for the ending of their ties with the close-knit communities of their youth, sometimes with the hope of a better life in their new homes, always with little choice. And as people settled away from inner London, so the seeds were sown for the post-war years of decline of these inner London communities, even before the plans for the rebirth of these areas could get underway. But this is part of the story of post-war London and not of London at war.

On a rainy day in August, Londoners celebrated the final end of the war, Victory over Japan. Their feelings that day were, as they had been on VE day just a few months earlier, ones primarily of relief that the suffering, the hardship, the destruction, the pain of war was at last over. As Londoners celebrated the end of the war, they also remembered the dead. In London, 30,000 civilians had died during the war and thousands more of the capital's young men had been killed in action on the military front. In a world war in which around forty million had been killed, the number may seem small, but for the very many Londoners who had lost members of their family or close friends, these feelings of loss were sometimes overwhelming. The memories would remain, sometimes deeply scarring people for the rest of their lives. Elsie Huntley recalls:

They had a party and I did attend, but my feelings were very sad, to think that I had lost my son through it all, and my mother. Because when my mother got the news about the doodlebug hitting us, she had a stroke and died. It took me a long time to get over it. That day is still very vivid in my mind and always will be.

Len Jones remembers:

Apart from the little injection of elation, I think the overall feeling for most of us was one of great sorrow because, for example, out of forty-seven blokes – school-boy pals, blokes I'd worked with – forty of them were killed, or they weren't any good any more mentally. The sadness there was so intense that it offset the fact that you won a war.

At that time I thought I was all right physically and mentally, but there was a time bomb in my brain that was going to blow out eventually and it did. I saw some buildings being pulled down more than twenty years later and I started shaking uncontrollably just like I had on that first night in the blitz. It brought back the destruction of those people that I'd known, disintegration of them, the total destruction of where I lived, all around me, the church that I'd been to and the school, my old place of work, all smashed to pieces, all in one night. And that to me was the end of the world, just a red sky. Fire, explosions, burning, smell, total destruction, that's what haunts, has haunted me ever since.

But on that last day of the war, Londoners had hope. While after VE day, people had worried that the new spirit of fairness and justice that had been born in the war would swiftly disappear, now Londoners were still buoyed by Labour's overwhelming election victory just a few weeks earlier. Londoners dreamed of new life rising out of the ashes, in which the best of the old would be preserved or rebuilt and the pre-war scars of poverty and squalor would be banished for ever.

The bombed-out wilderness that was the City of London after the war. There was a great hope that out of the ashes would rise a new and better life for everyone

FURTHER READING

It is difficult to recommend books that simply elaborate on our view of London at War, because our interpretation is, in places, quite different to that in most other books on the subject. Our interpretation is based on new research, and the serious reader might be interested in looking at some of the primary sources that we have used. First, there is the mass of material on the war held by the Public Record Office at Kew, in particular the Home Intelligence Daily Reports on morale in London (INFA/264 onwards). The best guide to these records is the Public Record Office Handbook, *The Second World War: A Guide to Documents in the P.R.O.* (H.M.S.O., 1972). Second, the Mass Observation Archive at the University of Sussex, which holds around a hundred file reports with material on London, is a mine of information on what ordinary people were thinking and doing in the capital. Third, there are the much neglected war memories of Londoners. We have interviewed or corresponded with several hundred who lived through the war, and our archive material will be deposited at the Imperial War Museum.

Two general books which we found extremely useful, though they are not specifically about London, are Angus Calder, *The People's War: Britain 1939–1945* (Granada, 1982) and Norman Longmate, *How We Lived Then: A History of Everyday Life During the Second World War* (Hutchinson, 1971). Both these books have comprehensive bibliographies on Britain in the Second World War. Also useful as an introduction is Arthur Marwick, *The Home Front* (Thames and Hudson, 1976). There have been many local studies on how particular boroughs fared during the war, and diaries and autobiographies which document personal experiences. The details are too numerous to list here, but information can be obtained from your local reference library. Below is a brief list of books we have found most useful for each chapter.

CHAPTER 1

On evacuation: Women's Group on Public Welfare, *Our Towns: A Close Up* (O.U.P., 1943), and National Federation of Women's Institutes, *Town Children Through Country Eyes* (1940). On propaganda and censorship: Ian McLaine, *The Ministry of Morale* (George Allen and Unwin, 1979), Marion Yass, *This Is Your War: Home Front Propaganda in the Second World War* (H.M.S.O., 1983) and Neil Stammers, *Civil Liberties in Britain during the Second World War* (Croom Helm, 1984). On the Phoney War: Mass Observation, *War Begins At Home* (Chatto and Windus, 1940), and E.S. Turner, *The Phoney War on the Home Front* (Michael Joseph, 1961). On internment: Peter and Leni Gillman, *Collar the Lot! How Britain Interned and Expelled Its Wartime Refugees* (Quartet, 1980) and Ronald Stent, *A Bespattered Page? The Internment of His Majesty's 'Most Loyal Enemy Aliens'* (André Deutsch, 1980). On invasion fears and preparations: Norman Longmate, *If Britain Had Fallen* (B.B.C. and Hutchinson, 1972), and *The Real Dad's Army: The Story of The Home Guard* (Hutchinson, 1974), and Laurence Thompson, *1940: Year of Legend, Year of History* (Collins, 1966).

CHAPTER 2

Tom Harrisson, *Living Through The Blitz* (Penguin, 1978), Leonard Mosley, *London Under Fire* (Pan, 1974), Constance Fitzgibbon, *The Blitz* (Windgate, 1957), Angus Calder *op. cit.*, Les Miller and Howard Bloch, *Black Saturday, The First Day of the Blitz: East London Memories of September 7th 1940* (T.H.A.P. Books, 1984), Neil Wallington, *Firemen at War: The Work of London's Fire Fighters in the Second World War* (David and Charles, 1981) and Stanley Rothwell, *Lambeth At War* (S.E.1 People's History Project, 1981).

CHAPTER 3

Richard Titmuss, *Problems of Social Policy* (Longmans, 1950), Ritchie Calder, *Carry on London* (English Universities, 1941) and *Lesson of London* (Secker and Warburg, 1941), Tom Harrisson *op. cit*, and David Johnson, *The City Ablaze* (William Kimber, 1980). The *Daily Herald* and the *Daily Worker* both have good coverage of the housing and sheltering crisis in the capital during the first months of the blitz.

CHAPTER 4

H.M.D. Parker, *Manpower: A Study of War-time Policy and Administration* (London H.M.S.O., 1957), Mass Observation, *People in Production: An Enquiry into British War Production* (John Murray, 1942), Raynes Minns, *Bombers and Mash: The Domestic Front 1939–45* (Virago, 1980), Penny Summerfield, *Women Workers in the Second World War* (Croom Helm, 1984), Norman Longmate, *How We Lived Then: A History of Everyday Life During the Second World War* (Hutchinson, 1971) and Guy Hartcup, *Code Name Mulberry: The Planning, Building and Operation of the Normandy Harbours* (David and Charles, 1977).

CHAPTER 5

Norman Longmate, *The Doodlebugs: The Story of the Flying Bombs* (Hutchinson 1981), and *Hitler's Rockets: The Story of the V2's* (Hutchinson, 1985), R.V. Jones, *Most Secret War: British Scientific Intelligence 1939–1945* (Hamish Hamilton, 1978), David Johnson, *V for Vengeance: The Second Battle of London* (William Kimber, 1981), Penny Summerfield *op. cit.*, and Edward Smithies, *Crime in Wartime: A Social History of Crime in World War 2* (George Allen and Unwin, 1982).

CHAPTER 6

Paul Addison, *The Road To 1945: British Politics and the Second World War* (Cape, 1975), Henry Pelling, *Britain and the Second World War* (Collins, 1970), R.B. McCallum and A. Readman, *The British General Election of 1945* (O.U.P., 1947), Ken Young and Patricia Garside, *Metropolitan London: Politics and Urban Change 1837–1981* (Edward Arnold, 1982), Felix Barker and Ralph Hyde, *London as it Might Have Been* (John Murray, 1982), Sir Leslie Abercrombie, *Greater London Plan 1944* (London, 1945), Norman Longmate, *The GIs: The Americans in Britain 1942–45* (Hutchinson, 1975) and *When We Won The War: The Story of Victory in Europe* (Hutchinson, 1977) and the essays by Marwick and Addison in Alan Sked and Chris Cook (eds.), *Crisis and Controversy, Essays in Honour of A.J.P. Taylor* (Macmillan, 1976).

INDEX